FROM
SUCCESS TO
FULFILLMENT

FROM
SUCCESS TO
FULFILLMENT

Applying the Wisdom of the Himalayan Masters

DEL PE

For general information on our other products and services, please contact our Sales Department within the United States at 1-800-352-6014, outside the United States at 1-936-273-9153, fax 1-936-273-9230 or Web site: www.mdpglobal.com.

Book design by Carolyn Wilder

First Edition Published: 2004

PRINTED IN THE UNITED STATES OF AMERICA

Library of Congress Control Number 2 0 0 4 1 0 4 2 4 0

ISBN 0-9717676-2-9

DISCLAIMER

This book presents the ideas, opinions, experiences and experiments of its author. This publication does not provide medical advice or diagnoses of health conditions. Readers, especially those with existing health conditions, should seek the advice of a medical professional before engaging in any of the techniques or practices in this book.

The author and publisher are not liable for any loss, health effect or other consequence of using or indirectly applying any technique or practice in this book.

This book is dedicated

To humanity on its path to success

To readers who are working for greater fulfillment

To those who inspire and teach others to succeed

To my family, co-workers and spiritual mentors

ACKNOWLEDGEMENTS

This book and its teachings are the result of many decades of my international travels, exploration and learning, many personal failures and successes, a few adversaries and countless friendships — but most of all, it is a product of team effort. Special thanks to:

- Jenna Wayne, my editor, who believed in this book and envisioned that it will help transform millions of executives and professionals

- Carolyn Wilder, my wife, who designed the book and made it appear better than I expected

- Kain Sanderson, the model for the exercises

- Susan Powell, the copy editor, whose recommendations made the book more practical

- Suzanne Jarvis and the GLOCEN and ESOCEN trainers for their continued support in the spreading of these teachings

- Joe Robbins for his special photography skills

- Rick Frishman and David Hahn from Planned Television Arts for challenging me to write this book, thank you!

To my clients around the world for being living proof that the book's success and self-fulfillment strategies really work.

In addition, I am grateful to my parents, children and family for their full support and belief in my mission.

I am deeply grateful to MCKS, my earlier spiritual mentor, for his advanced spiritual teachings and to my Himalayan Masters and my other mentors for their priceless spiritual guidance and training.

CONTENTS

TABLE OF DIAGRAMS AND ILLUSTRATIONS

INTRODUCTION

---◆---

Are you ready to take a unique trip to the shores of success and the land of fulfillment? Don't be surprised if this book is totally different from any other book about success you may have read before!

From Success to Fulfillment brings a unique perspective on performance, success and fulfillment that incorporates the Eastern Wisdom of the Himalayan Masters.

So, let's start our journey with an important question: Is there something beyond success? You bet there is!

Success is getting what you want, but do all successful people end up liking what they get? Many professionals around the world work so hard to get what they want: recognition, a satisfying career, a family, luxurious vacations, material possessions like a nice home, an expensive car, maybe a yacht or jet.

But if success is a main goal, why do so many people achieve their dreams only to find that their success isn't completely satisfying? Why do they discover that at some point their success can ultimately be very lonely? Because many people sacrifice their entire lives for their success without ever stopping to question whether there might be something more or whether the success is really worth it after sacrificing important areas of life like family, health or spiritual principles.

For the first time in modern history, we can say that many people are acknowledging their "failure of success". With intense pressure to perform, especially in an economic climate of increasing competition and globalization, increasing numbers of roles to juggle, higher levels of stress and the loneliness that can come with incomplete success, people everywhere need practical ways to be totally successful and self-fulfilled without sacrificing health, family, spirituality and social value in life.

Some who experience the failure of success wake up to the fact that there is something beyond success because life gives them a "big hammer" to make them consider shifting course: a major illness, a divorce, a child addicted to drugs, a job layoff...It's in the moments when life delivers surprises we can't control or solve easily that people sometimes are finally forced to stop pursuing success long enough to contemplate what really matters.

I was lucky to learn this concept of something beyond success early on living in Asia, where I spent my early life. As I experienced life's opportunities and lessons, I set out on a journey to discover the meaning of life and who I am in this world. I was very blessed early in life to study with great authentic, nurturing, advanced Sages from different spiritual lineages as spiritual mentors, some of whom had been successful businesspeople themselves. They taught me the fundamentals and true regimen of advanced human faculty development, patiently facilitated my inner training and fostered my early spiritual education, which led to a different understanding of success and fulfillment.

To these teachers — and as I've discovered in my own life — success isn't just measured in riches and material comfort. It's not just about performance and meeting other people's expectations. We said earlier that success is getting what you want, but according to the Eastern Wisdom, true success comes from dynamically satisfying other essential things in life.

Financial freedom and material comfort are good. Performing well at whatever you do and feeling valued for your work are important. Creating excellence through positive competition helps build dynamic momentum. But this is not all there is to success. According to the Eastern Wisdom and my own experience, momentum is internally-generated. Success is self-defined. Real success requires a balanced life where all the aspects of who you are – physical, emotional, mental and spiritual – are nourished with healthy non-physical and physical diets. To the Himalayan Masters, if any part of you is "starved", your success is incomplete.

When I finally found my advanced teachers, I had been a very successful engineer and businessperson for more than 12 years. I spent most of my time working in the Middle East for the world's largest oil-producing company. At the age of 24, I was the Chief Karate Master of one the biggest martial arts organizations in Saudi Arabia, and I trained many champions.

I experienced success, but I sensed that there was something more, and this sensing led me to a new path. On this path, I haven't rejected the idea of material success or given away all I own. I didn't disappear into the Himalayas to spend my life meditating in seclusion, though I was offered that opportunity. What I did choose to do was emerge from my spiritual training with a deeper understanding of inner values and advanced human faculties to help professionals everywhere perform even better in every area of life with material and spiritual balance.

So what's the secret? What lies beyond success? Fulfillment. We said success is getting what you want, but fulfillment is enjoying what you have through a balanced life achieved with integrity. If you work so hard over a lifetime to get what you want, don't you deserve to enjoy the fruits of your labor? Don't your family and loved ones deserve to have you around for many years to share in your success? Don't you deserve to enjoy life more with less stress?

This book is all about helping you design your destiny for both success and fulfillment. With practical principles and techniques that apply Eastern Wisdom and Western practicality, every chapter gives you a concrete roadmap to transform success into fulfillment while maximizing your performance and balancing your life.

By using the tools offered in this book, your success can be more sustained and satisfying, and you can experience self-fulfillment implementing a more integrated path and bigger vision in life. The wisdom of the teachings in this book has been gathered from my years of living in and studying many cultures and traveling to more than 40 countries researching, validating and teaching global models of success. The practical strategies in the different chapters are products of my integrated experience as an engineer, businessperson, martial arts master and teacher of Eastern philosophies and training with four enlightened spiritual mentors who gave me some of the secrets of self-fulfillment known as part of the Eastern Wisdom found in the Himalayas.

May this book serve as your lighthouse, compass and map on your journey to the shores of success and the land of fulfillment.

- Del Pe

CHAPTER I

FROM SUCCESS TO FULFILLMENT:
A HIGHER PATH IN LIFE

Whether you are a seasoned leader or a new profession-al, young or old, male or female, American, Asian or from another culture, there is a universal model of suc-cess and fulfillment. Beneath our differences, there are even stronger similarities, and herein lies the bright future of humanity.

Most if not all people along the path from success to fulfillment need to satisfy five most important areas in life. They also need to develop and balance three divine human qualities of will-power, love and creative intelligence. We call these three integrated quali-ties the Triangle of Success and Fulfillment, a universal model for a happier, healthier and more balanced life that will be discussed thor-oughly with case studies in this chapter and chapter 2.

Spiritual teachers like the Himalayan Masters have recognized and understood some aspects of this universal model for thousands of years. A practical, systematic understanding is now available in this book, leading to a new opportunity to bring this Eastern Wisdom to the West in a more modern form that integrates a Western objective approach.

Understanding and applying the universal model is what is need-ed for sustained success and fulfillment in the professional world today and to be able to achieve in a few years what most people cannot achieve in a lifetime.

Seeking Success In The Modern World

Never before have people invested so much in success. Currently, personal development is estimated to be a more than 7 billion-dollar industry in the United States[1]. It is projected to grow at least 9.1 percent per year[2] through 2005. Why is this happening now?

First, as corporations have downsized, affecting training and education programs, people have increasingly turned to educating themselves through seminars, books, audio programs and other self-study tools. Academic learning continues to be important, but is less and less a predictor of success in the "real world".

Second, some people have not only invested so much time and effort in their work, but have also sacrificed their families, health and life's principles to sustain material and professional success. This is a high price to pay for success, so many people are now giving more attention to achieving work-life balance.

Efficient ways of employing technology and practical use of resources have been the major focus of success. But these bring only partial success. Fulfillment means integrating life experience, wisdom, a deeper, more systematic knowledge of oneself and others and a practical, grounded approach to all areas of life. These are also important additional needed ingredients for success.

For most people, however, success isn't enough. Success is getting what you want, which is usually temporary. True fulfillment is enjoying what you have, but it should not emphasize a static balanced life. Rather, it should emphasize an ongoing balancing of priorities in all areas of life and dynamically fulfilling new evolving responsibilities.

As we achieve outer success and goals, a natural next step is to turn inward, looking for more fulfillment and meaning in life. We may ask questions like, "Why am I here"?, "What's my next real purpose"?, "Why do I have it all and still feel like there's something more"? and "Why can I run a successful business, leading 10,000 employees, but fail to manage a small family with 3 children successfully"?

Your success as a family, our success as a society,
depends not on what happens in the White House,
but on what happens inside your house.

Barbara Bush, Former US First Lady

Why Transform Success Into Fulfillment?

Success without fulfillment is only half the path to your complete achievement. Performing, achieving and getting more things, positions and recognition without being able to enjoy what you have and contributing to your greater purpose often leads to the "failure of success" with its sense of inner emptiness.

SUCCESS is...

- Meeting goals and getting what you want

- Making a difference

- Good personal or professional relationships

- Job security with good pay

- Fame and reputation

- Being liked and admired

- Comfortable material life and financial freedom

- A good education

- Consistent job promotions and salary increases

Whereas,

FAILURE OF SUCCESS is...

- Heart attack, paralysis or other debilitating illness at a young age due to over-work

- Unfulfilled family life and failed relationships

- Loneliness due to lack of relationships

- Financial failure and losing companies after decades of success

- Goals achieved, but poor health due to vices like smoking, alcoholism, drug addiction, gambling and/or sexually risky behavior

- Ending up poor after a lifetime of hard work

- Lack of spiritual meaning after achieving fame and glory

- Top executives causing severe damage and suffering to others due to poor business decisions or lack of integrity

- Dying rich without making a difference in the world

- Becoming a multimillionaire at the expense of virtues

- Dying abandoned by loved ones

FULFILLMENT IS...

- Enjoying what you have achieved with a life of integrity

- All areas of life are balanced with sustained health and vitality

- A life of service that leaves a legacy

- A sense that you would like to do your current work or service for a lifetime and even for free because you have found your sense of purpose

- Satisfying and harmonious relationships not only limited to family, but beyond

- Overall sense of well-being, inner peace and inner joy

- Balanced material and spiritual life

- A life guided by values more associated with inner aspects of life

THERE ARE FOUR PATHS IN LIFE:

1. A successful life without fulfillment
2. A successful life transformed into self-fulfillment
3. A successful life ending in failure
4. A life of neither success nor fulfillment

Which path are you currently on?

The beauty of life is that we as human beings can choose which path to take. But would it be easier to choose your direction in life with navigating maps and tools?

This book offers you just these types of maps and tools. It provides a systematic practical path equipped with new tools, advanced faculty development and inner values to help you achieve total success and transform that success into fulfillment.

THE 5 MOST IMPORTANT AREAS OF LIFE

We have found working with clients in many different countries and cultures that success leading to fulfillment is sustainable if you balance the five most important areas of life. Over-investment or under-investment in any of these areas creates predictable blind spots, challenges and obstacles — manifesting either today or in the future as a cause of failure.

Let's look at the five most important areas of life that are applicable for any culture:

Figure 1

Family and Home

Family and Home refers to all of your roles, goals, activities and tasks with family and maintaining your home. Being at home, nurturing family relationships, errands, paying home bills, family planning, meals with family, family vacation, etc. fit here.

Career and Work

Career and Work refers to all of your roles, goals, activities and tasks related to your career and work. The normal work activities, plus commuting time, work-related organization and planning, professional self-education, etc. fit here. If you are a student, your educational activities would be in this category.

Health and Recreation

Health and Recreation refers to all of your roles, goals, activities and tasks related to maintaining your health and enjoying your life with recreational time. Exercise, sleep, hobbies, attending a health-related seminar, going to the movies, sports, etc. fit here. Activities like movies and sports can be combined with family time or social life for synchronized time management. This time-saver is discussed further in this chapter and chapter 2.

Social Life and Environmental Contribution

Social Life and Environmental Contribution is divided into the two aspects of social life and environmental contribution. Social Life refers to all of your roles, goals, activities and tasks related to socializing with friends without contributing to the community whereas Environmental Contribution is a mark of a more developed person, demonstrated by participating in environmental improvement. For instance, time with friends would fit into Social Life. Volunteer work, membership in or funding of charitable and philanthropic organizations, etc. would fit in Environmental Contribution. A more fulfilled person usually has a bigger vision of life and a sense of being able to contribute on a greater scale. You can gauge a person's development by knowing how much contribution to society and the world they have made.

SPIRITUAL LIFE

Spiritual Life refers to all of your roles, goals, activities and tasks related to growing spiritually. For some, this means going to church or supporting religious projects. For others, it means meditating or practicing yoga. For still others, it means applying their best skills and talents to bettering humanity and finding more meaning in life. Whatever form your spiritual life takes, it is the true key to lasting success and fulfillment. In a more evolved person, the spiritual life starts to encompass and integrate all the other areas of life.

When you study how these five areas are balanced or imbalanced in your own life, areas of over- or under-investment become obvious, and your blind spots and potential obstacles are easy to identify and predict.

In this process, it is better to know your blind spots and potential obstacles ahead of time to manage them properly. There's no need to fear succeeding at the end through some mistakes or degrees of failure. Life goes on, and it is through a dynamic, ongoing balancing of goals and priorities in the five areas that self-fulfillment can be achieved.

To be elated at success and disappointed at failure
is to be the child of circumstances;
how can such a one be called master of himself?
Chinese Proverb

Let's look at some case studies to understand how this works.

Areas of Life Case Studies

To illustrate the key points throughout this book, I will share some of my clients' life stories.

Case Study 1:
The Price of Excessive Ambition Sacrificing Other Areas

John Claire, a sales executive who is married with three children, makes 20 international business trips annually and works an average of 12 hours a day, five days a week when he's in the office. He has no real interest in spirituality although he does attend a few days of church services at Easter and Christmas. John is always too tired to socialize with friends and relatives except during his wife's and children's birthdays. He has no sense of community service and no interest in environmental concerns. He sleeps an average of five hours per day and plays golf two Saturdays a month as recreation. Most of his time is spent with clients, including some weekends.

Here's how John Claire spends his life based on summarizing his five areas of life in our coaching chart:

John Claire's Areas of Life

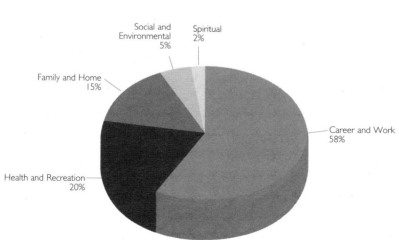

Social and Environmental 5%
Spiritual 2%
Family and Home 15%
Career and Work 58%
Health and Recreation 20%

John clearly over-invests in his Career and Work, but starves time and effort in his Environmental Contribution area and his Spiritual Life. His family time is quite stretched. His chart shows that the lack of time spent in the areas of Social Life and Environmental Contribution and Spiritual Life prevents him from enjoying a deeper sense of purpose in life, which triggers a sense of emptiness or meaninglessness.

If he continues to follow the same schedule, it is possible that he will get fast job promotions and higher income, but in the long run, he might end up with an unfulfilled marriage, family life and spirituality. With John's chart, we can evaluate a potential "failure of success" in his future if his distribution of priorities is not rectified and his life not put into balance.

Preoccupation with non-essentials and ignoring of urgent important things in life is a major cause of the failure of success.

CASE STUDY 2:
THE CONSEQUENCES OF STARVING YOUR CAREER LIFE

Let's look at another typical case. Maria Isabel Suarez is a bank executive who, after three years of marriage, has agreed with her wealthy husband to stay at home. They do not have children. She spends most of her time managing the house, playing with her dog, watching TV and taking good care of their garden.

Her husband, a bank CEO, travels frequently and works 10 to 14 hours a day. He works an average of six days a week, including business social events that he attends alone. Maria Isabel socializes with friends and does community service. Her boredom has led her to join a spiritual circle of meditators and yoga practitioners who attend weekly seminars with her. Maria Isabel has become health-conscious and eats well. She sleeps an average of 10 hours a day.

Estimating her year's expenditure of time and resources, Maria Isabel's five areas of life chart looks like this:

Maria Isabel's Areas of Life

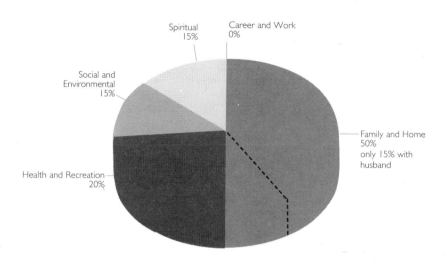

While this bright, educated and ambitious former executive endeavors to fill her time with meaningful activities, she feels an emptiness much of the time. Using the five areas of life chart, it is easy to identify the sources of her unhappiness and lack of fulfillment. Maria Isabel does not have enough time with her husband, and they do not have substantial shared activities to fulfill their marriage, especially since they can't have children.

She is clearly bored and not challenged mentally through a career. Therefore, she feels something important is missing in terms of professional development. However, she is enjoying a healthy physical lifestyle, and her friends and spiritual peers love her. Maria Isabel is also admired by the people she serves through her community work. She is successful in many ways, but is having issues with her marriage. Personal and professional balance is the major problem blocking her path to total success and self-fulfillment.

CHARTING YOUR LIFE

Let's study your own life. You can use a sample list of activities like the one below to calculate your time and life expenditures every month or every year.

Self-Assessment of Your Activities and Time Allocations

Percent of total time = Time allocated for activity divided by total hours of that week or month

Total time:

1 week:	168 hours
28-day month:	672 hours
29-day month:	696 hours
30-day month:	720 hours
31-day month:	744 hours

How do you spend your time? Include the number of hours and the percentages for each area of life. The allocations in the five areas of life added up should total 100%.

Description

Estimated
Time Allocations
Hours and Percentage

A. Family and Home

**Weekly, Monthly
or
Yearly Estimates**

1. Activity with partner/spouse   _____
2. Activity with children   _____
3. Common activity with spouse/partner/
    children (time while not sleeping)   _____
4. Activity with parents or relatives   _____
5. Regular home chores   _____
6. Errands   _____
7. Financial and technical home planning   _____

8. Family vacations   _____
9. Family-related seminars   _____
10. Miscellaneous   _____
                                    Sub-total   _____
                        Percent of total time   _____

B. Career and Work

**Weekly, Monthly
or
Yearly Estimates**

1. Work-related regular activities   _____
2. Travel time to and from work   _____
3. Travel time outside regular office work   _____
4. Career or skill development within work   _____
5. Career or skill development outside work   _____
6. Extra planning and organizing   _____
7. Socializing for business   _____
8. Miscellaneous   _____
                                    Sub-total   _____
                        Percent of total time   _____

C. Social Life and Environmental Contribution

**Weekly, Monthly
or
Yearly Estimates**

1. Purely social interactions   _____
2. Environmental or community services   _____
3. Planning/organizing for social activities   _____
4. Planning/organizing for environmental activities   _____
5. Miscellaneous   _____
                                    Sub-total   _____
                        Percent of total time   _____

D. Spiritual Life Activities

**Weekly, Monthly
or
Yearly Estimates**

1. Religious practices _____
2. Spiritual practices _____
3. Spiritual seminars and projects _____
4. Meditation for spiritual growth _____
5. Study for inner development _____
6. Spiritual group work _____
7. Planning/organizing for spiritual activities _____
8. Spiritual retreats _____
9. Miscellaneous _____

Sub-total _____

Percent of total time _____

E. Health and Recreation

**Weekly, Monthly
or
Yearly Estimates**

1. Rest and sleep _____
2. Physical exercises _____
3. Extra chores to improve health _____
4. Study to improve health _____
5. Seminars to improve health _____
6. Recreation and sports _____
7. Vacations for health _____
8. Preparing and eating healthy meals _____
9. Planning/organizing for health _____
10. Hobbies (reading, camping, movies) _____
11. Miscellaneous _____

Sub-total _____

Percent of total time

Analyze Your Results

Now let's use the results from your self-assessment above to chart your life and time expenditures below. Fill out areas of life below with your percentages and draw your life's chart in the circle.

Your Distribution of Time in All Areas

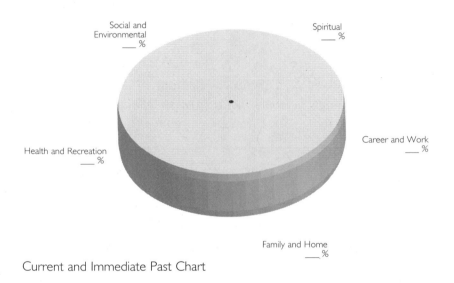

Social and Environmental ___ %

Spiritual ___ %

Career and Work ___ %

Health and Recreation ___ %

Family and Home ___ %

Current and Immediate Past Chart

Next Steps

How do you like (or dislike) your chart? Where are you spending time excessively or under-investing your time and effort? By studying and evaluating your chart, you can determine your areas of strength and weakness, including your potential seeds of failure. It is like having a "vitamin deficiency", with a need to add "time supplements" to bring back your balance. It can be done this way: Add more time, effort and focus in starved areas and subtract your time and non-essential activities where there is over-investment.

Dynamic balancing in life requires focus and more time in certain areas. Therefore, your chart every month should not be static in the sense of equal percentage of time expenditure in all the areas since it will be affected by how the most urgent important goals shift monthly or periodically.

For example, if you are starting a new company, your Career and Work will have more time than the Social Life and Environmental Contribution or even family life for a while, but this situation should not last for years.

Another example is someone who has just had a baby: The Family and Home area receives more time and focus, but Career and Work should not be sacrificed after a few years.

> *Life should be a continuous balancing of urgent important priorities, not a fixed set of scales.*

Most of my clients and students who take my Life Planning and Time Management seminars are surprised and dismayed by what they see when we first chart their areas of life. Many of them are over-worked, burned out and lack time for their health, which causes many illnesses. At the same time, they are under-invested in their families and do not serve their communities or have a satisfying, fulfilling spiritual life.

The good news is that my seminars and coaching sessions help clients see options to carefully plan for a lifestyle that brings more balance and fulfillment to their personal and professional lives.

CHARTING YOUR BALANCED LIFE:
The Power to Pilot Your Destiny

How can you do this? Estimate a reasonable time distribution for your five most important areas that you think can bring balance back into your life every month in every year. Then draw your chart, and do your best to implement it by designing a plan and schedule that satisfies your new life.

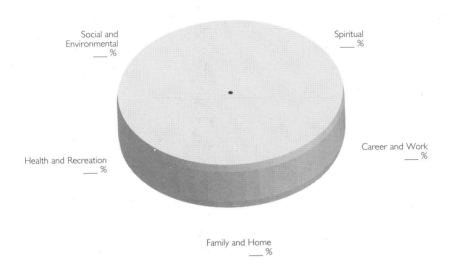

Your New Distribution of Time
To Balance Your Areas of Life

Your New Chart = Your New Life

The beauty and advantage of using the strategy of charting your areas of life and evaluating how you spend your time every month is to be able to identify your blind spots and the potential seeds of failure before they present a problem or crisis.

Isn't it inspiring to know that you have the power to regulate your future with tools available to change your lifestyle, design your plans properly and balance your expenditure of time and effort in the five areas, thus piloting your destiny? Yes, you do have the choice and capability to create the matrix of your future life and transform your success into fulfillment.

ROADMAP TO MAKE THE CHANGES YOU WANT

There are several strategies to maximize your productivity and performance in all of life's five areas to achieve more in less time while maintaining balance. Try following these solutions and guidelines:

1. Manage your time with synchronicity.

Synchronized time management goes far beyond multi-tasking because it integrates a variety of essential activities so more can be accomplished in less time. Synchronized time management is required to become more effective at managing goals and balancing all areas of life.

For example, on the same vacation, couples or partners can attend family-related and spiritual seminars together while enjoying each other's company, followed by recreational activities. Children can participate, too, when they're old enough. The family members can also share in a common community service that promotes environmental contribution and embodies spiritual values. Some people may change careers so they can work in jobs that directly benefit the environment, local community or international service programs while promoting spiritual enhancement. If you are not finding fulfillment in your career and it is difficult to change jobs, plan to build time into your five areas of life chart to volunteer for a social or environmental cause that interests you. Thus:

Career/Work + Spiritual Life/Service + Social Life
and Environmental Contribution =
One Connected, Synchronized Goal/Activity/Result

2. Share your life.

Design a shared vision, common goals and important activities with your family or life partner. Business trips can be planned along with family vacations and holidays to combine business, leisure and family activities. Partnership among family members in commercial or business ventures can be beneficial to support shared vision and common goals. This can be a solution for spouses who are unable to go back to regular office work or their previous careers.

3. Support a good cause.

Use your assets to financially support spiritual or social projects that further evolution and total well-being. You can go one step higher by becoming a volunteer or member of the board of directors for these types of organizations or projects to express your avocation. This expression of service can even be therapeutic if you are not enjoying your job or career.

4. Make a big difference.

Integrate the areas of life with greater usefulness. Develop a planning criterion for you, your family and co-workers not only to have synchronized time management, but also to multi-purpose goals and activities that have greater usefulness to yourself and others.

Many fulfilled philanthropists are now engaged in social entrepreneurship, making a big difference in the lives of millions while enjoying greater tax benefits and creating a legacy with a life of continued abundance. Most people who are legends have incorporated Environmental Contribution as part of their spiritual responsibility. Not all of them are religious, but they are spiritual. Throughout history, people who used their lives to make lasting contributions to others have been remembered as saints. Today, these practical philanthropic businesspeople and entrepreneurs are legendary world servers. Many are modern saints in the making.

CASE STUDY 3:
BALANCED AND FULFILLED LIFE

Let's look at another case of the more balanced and sychronized life of Oscar Wayne, a wealthy business executive who transformed into a philanthropist at age 50. He is not just providing funds to an orphanage, but also serves as a member of their Board of Trustees. A few Sundays every month, Oscar also coaches the young orphans in basketball and invites the orphanage personnel to dinner.

Oscar wasn't always so balanced and philanthropic. Pushed from a very young age by his parents to get top grades in school and to compete in alpine skiing at the Olympic level, Oscar did not experience a normal childhood.

His parents sent him to a private boarding school in the mountains when he was 6 years old so he could start training for the Olympics. Any "spare time" he had when he wasn't studying was spent training for skiing daily.

Because he studied and trained so hard at such a young age, Oscar became intensely competitive and serious. He had no time for friends, so he didn't develop normal friendships and social skills. He was dynamic because of his physical strength, good looks and mental intelligence, and the confidence he got from his skiing abilities made him influential with people, even though he wasn't very pleasant. Since many people just wanted to be around him because he was training for the Olympics, he learned how to manipulate people to get what he wanted.

All this came to an end, though, when at 20, he had a major skiing accident that ended his athletic career instantly. Sent into a deep depression and identity crisis, Oscar dropped out of university and buried his pain in alcohol, cigarettes, recreational drug use and casual sexual liaisons.

At the end of the year, Oscar was running out of money and needed to find something to do with himself. The competitive aspect of business intrigued him as a replacement for skiing, and he decided to invest his energies in making his fortune.

With the powers of focus and visualization he learned in skiing, Oscar started his own commercial real estate company in Silicon Valley, California during its first technology boom and made a fortune very fast. He invested shrewdly in other businesses and continued to build his wealth.

As he built this wealth he needed to hire people to help him. He paid them well because he thought this was the only way to keep them loyal. He had a reputation for being ruthless, manipulative and explosive, making demands for performance that few could achieve.

At 34, Oscar had a car accident while driving drunk. He quit drinking overnight as a result, but he continued to smoke, became more stressed and pushed his employees to work even harder.

When he was 35, he met his current wife. They were married two years later. From the beginning, Oscar invested more time in his business than in his relationship. After they had children, his long work hours and frequent trips away from home strained their relationship further.

When Oscar turned 48, his life changed completely. While driving home late from work one night, he suffered a heart attack and had the second major car accident in his life. This accident, combined with a heart attack at what he considered to be such a young age, finally forced him to slow down while recuperating from heart surgery and the reconstruction of the leg that was damaged 28 years before in his skiing accident.

The doctors told him his life depended on quitting smoking and reducing stress immediately as a way of life.

Through a friend of his wife, Oscar heard about and attended a life-balancing seminar, which introduced him to the five areas of life philosophy. He started working with a spiritual mentor, who helped him with his areas of life chart. Oscar also received services from the same mentor to quit his addictions and live healthier.

During the mentoring, Oscar discovered that many of his negative behaviors were a result of his extreme focus on performance stemming from his childhood. He recognized the imbalances created by a very competitive attitude sacrificing his family, social life and spiritual values.

His mentor advised him that using his wealth to support philanthropic work, especially work supporting orphans and abandoned children, would help heal his own issues of insufficient emotional nurturing.

As a result of the mentoring, Oscar's life has changed completely in the two years since his heart attack.

At work, he remains the president of his company. He has become a master delegator, working only seven hours a day, five days a week. His wife works with him as the Sales Manager. They go home together often and sometimes go to the gym together on weekends. On Wednesdays, the whole family enjoys playing tennis before they go to the movies.

Oscar's wife and mother-in-law are active in their religion and also do yoga spiritual practices, so he joins them every Sunday for spiritual study and meditation. Their two teenaged sons join them as well.

This is his chart and the tabulation of his time expenditures:

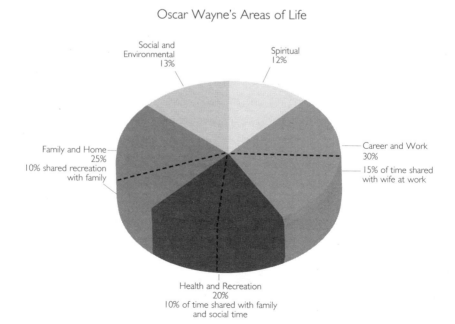

Oscar Wayne's Areas of Life

Social and Environmental 13%

Spiritual 12%

Family and Home 25%
10% shared recreation with family

Career and Work 30%
15% of time shared with wife at work

Health and Recreation 20%
10% of time shared with family and social time

Balanced Areas of Life with Synchronized Time Management

With his life balanced in all five areas through mentoring, Oscar has finally achieved fulfillment and lives every day with deep appreciation for his family, his work, his opportunity to use his wealth to help children and for the spiritual fulfillment he receives from helping others.

The most successful people are those who are able to go the extra miles in effort and spend more time doing the most important things that bring the greatest value to life while maintaining balance.

Is there really such thing as total success and fulfillment?

As an example of total success and self-fulfillment, Mother Teresa's five areas of life chart looks approximately like this:

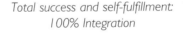

Total success and self-fulfillment:
100% Integration

Synchronized purpose, goals and activities working for humanity's upliftment, considering all of humanity as her entire family and her whole career, social life and environmental contribution part of spiritual life

Total Success and Fulfillment

How can one achieve total success and fulfillment? Understanding where you invest your time is the first step. This book will not only guide you on synchronizing your time and areas of life, but also gives you new tools and strategies to make your life easier, healthier and happier.

This book shows you how to make adjustments in your life to transform success to fulfillment by providing a practical understanding of:

1. The Success and Fulfillment Triangle: A Universal Model
2. The Secrets of Your Power Centers
3. How to Develop Your Will-Power and Vitality Fast
4. How Love Fuels Success and Fulfillment
5. How Your Creative Intelligence Can Make You a Mental Powerhouse
6. 8 Core Values to Balance Your Material and Spiritual Life
7. A Special Meditation to Heal and Empower Your Life

Each subsequent chapter in this book offers quick and practical techniques you can apply immediately to maximize your performance and enhance your ability to succeed and be fulfilled. Combining Eastern Wisdom and Western practicality, there's even a special meditation designed for today's busy professionals that can create breakthroughs in your life. This book concludes with practical weekly schedules and strategies that can help you every day on your path from success to fulfillment.

CHAPTER 2

THE SUCCESS AND FULFILLMENT TRIANGLE:
A UNIVERSAL MODEL

───────────◆───────────

The Universal Model of complete success and lasting fulfillment involves three qualities of life that need to be applied, integrated and balanced. These three qualities can be demonstrated as positive human attitudes, aptitudes and inner values or virtues.

THE SUCCESS AND FULFILLMENT TRIANGLE

Let's first study the three qualities that comprise the success and fulfillment triangle:

1. Will-power
2. Love
3. Creative intelligence

By observing the progress brought by evolution, you can see that nature demonstrates the principle of the triangle: In order to create new forms, there is a need to destroy the old, obsolete forms using power. Then new forms and consciousness are constructed using creative intelligence. After that, they are preserved through love. These qualities are expressed in some countries through seasons like winter (destruction), spring (creation) and summer (preservation).

Many spiritual and religious traditions emphasize these universal qualities of success and fulfillment in their teachings as follows: omnipotence (will-power), all-lovingness (love) and omniscience (creative intelligence). In Christianity, will-power, love and creative intelligence are represented by the trinity of the Father (will-power), the Son (love) and the Holy Spirit (creative intelligence) – three divine qualities in one God.

Hinduism also believes in three expressions of divinity through a trinity: Shiva, the Divine Destroyer, Vishnu, the Divine Preserver and Brahma, the Divine Creator.

The triangles representing will-power, love and creative intelligence in different religions and traditions throughout the world demonstrate an underlying universality of the potential of the three qualities in people.

This universal principle is not just limited to religions and spiritual traditions. It can be seen throughout creation as follows:

WILL-POWER	LOVE	CREATIVE INTELLIGENCE
Equivalents to Will-Power Quality:	Equivalents to Love Quality:	Equivalents to Creative Intelligence Quality:
Father	Son	Holy Ghost
Shiva	Vishnu	Brahma
Destruction	Preservation	Creation
Winter	Summer	Spring
Protons	Neutrons	Electrons
Alkali	Salt	Acid
Nitrogen	Oxygen	Hydrogen

TRINITIES IN DIFFERENT SPIRITUAL TRADITIONS

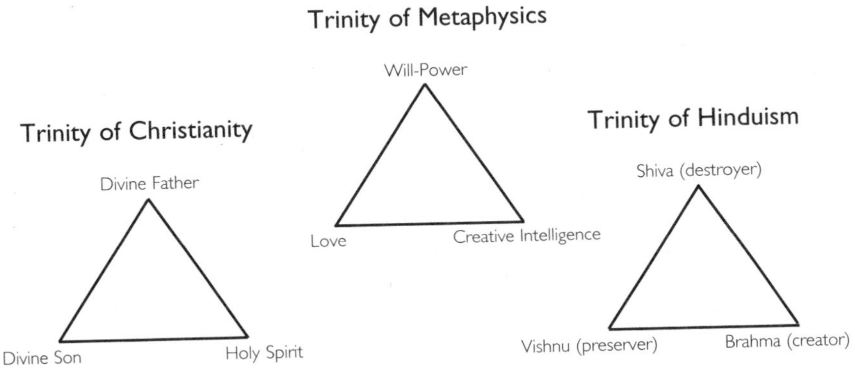

Trinity of Metaphysics

Trinity of Christianity

Trinity of Hinduism

Will-Power

Love   Creative Intelligence

Divine Father

Divine Son   Holy Spirit

Shiva (destroyer)

Vishnu (preserver)   Brahma (creator)

Figure 2

Let's define the three qualities and Triangle for Success and Fulfillment further:

WILL-POWER can be expressed as the powers of stamina, vitality, strength, endurance and persistence. Will-power can also be used for constructive destruction like that of the natural forces. Vitality and discipline are developed in parallel with the virtue of will-power. Discipline and will-power will be discussed in more detail in chapter 7.

LOVE can be expressed as the qualities of compassion, understanding, inclusiveness and joy. The virtues expressing love are benevolence, altruism and sacrifice. See chapter 7 for a deeper discussion of these virtues.

CREATIVE INTELLIGENCE demonstrates through the powers of the mind, innovation, creativity, arts, science and technology. The main virtue required to concretize creative intelligence is objectivity and practicality. This is also discussed in chapter 7.

INTEGRATED POWER

There is actually a fourth quality for success and fulfillment: the integration of will-power, love and creative intelligence. This integration requires all of the above virtues, as well as group consciousness and good health at physical, energetic, emotional, mental and spiritual levels. The integration of will-power, love and creative intelligence creates the potential for lasting success and fulfillment.

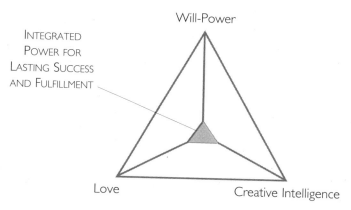

Will-Power

INTEGRATED
POWER FOR
LASTING SUCCESS
AND FULFILLMENT

Love

Creative Intelligence

Figure 3

The ability to become fully successful and fulfilled, and to sustain this state, depends largely on how much of the three qualities of will-power, love and creative intelligence can be mastered one-by-one or in combination to create integrated or synthesized power. The more integrated these qualities in you, the more success and fulfillment you can have. Let's take the example of leadership to see how each of these qualities is expressed practically.

There are four major kinds of leaders:

I. Leaders with Will-Power

Leaders with will-power and political influence are rulers with authority over nations and organizations. Will-power sustains focus on the vision and purpose of life. People with strong will-power are naturally born with leadership capabilities and strength.

2. Leaders with a Good Heart

The most motivating and inspiring leaders are those who have the power of the heart or love. They are most loved and adored by their followers, like the Christ or the Buddha and other founders of religions. More evolved people with great love are also endowed with wisdom.

3. Leaders with a Good Mind

Leaders with creative intelligence have the power of money, resources, arts and technology. In our modern society, the richest people tend to fit in this category.

4. Integrated Leaders

These are leaders with a combination of two or three of the above types or qualities. They are the most successful and fulfilled and can thrive in any era, economy or adversity. Among them, you'll find leaders with a good heart and mind and great will-power.

A person's success and fulfillment tend to be less balanced or long-lasting when one or more of the three qualities of will-power, love and creative intelligence is under-developed or not expressed. A person who applies and integrates all three qualities tends to have bigger vision and better results in life.

Someone who lacks the three qualities or who has not integrated them yet tends to have certain blind spots, traps and obstacles that can create fears and blockages to performing at their best. For example, there are inspirational loving leaders who do not enjoy material abundance.

Likewise, some very creative, wealthy, successful leaders are sickly and don't have stable family relationships. Also, many strong political leaders have will-power and social influence, but are not that prosperous. Some are lonely in bad relationships.

ASSESS YOURSELF

You are about to experience the first Know Yourself-Develop Yourself exercise in this book. Every time we introduce a principle, we give you the opportunity to know yourself better according to that principle and set 6-month targets to develop aspects that can dramatically transform your performance and success.

Unless otherwise noted, you will be using the following rating key.

KNOW YOURSELF-DEVELOP YOURSELF KEY

4 = Fully developed
3 = Well developed
2 = Partially developed
1 = Just starting to develop
0 = Not developed at all

Let's assess the current development of your Success and Fulfillment Triangle and set a new development goal every sixth months.

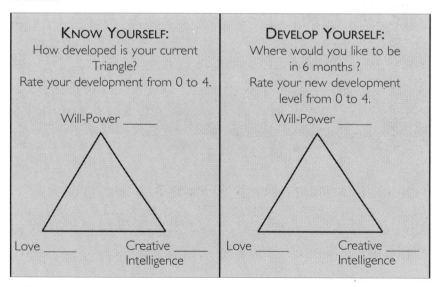

How can you improve your Triangle and qualities? Chapters 4-9 give you specific strategies, techniques and schedules.

General Tabulation of the Success and Fulfillment Triangle

Quality	Inherent Virtues	Results Naturally Achieved Through The Quality
Will-power	Will-power and stamina Discipline and constancy Persistence and determination Fearlessness Speed in achieving results Focus on vision/purpose	Political powers Material success Strong natural leadership style Most respected people
Love	Benevolence Altruism Virtue of sacrifice Inclusiveness, harmony and peace	Charismatic powers Happiness and wealth Success in relationships Most inspiring leadership Most loved people
Creative Intelligence	Objectivity and practicality Innovativeness and creativity Ability to organize and structure business Aptitude for arts, science and technology	Financial powers Material success Creative and strategic leadership based on expertise Most liked people

Top Qualities of Fully Successful People

What top qualities do most successful people share regardless of culture, age, profession or gender? Let's discuss them one at a time.

Will-Power and Vitality
Most fully successful people have great will-power and vitality to

overcome their obstacles, materialize their goals faster and finish what they start. The virtue of will-power and vitality is the key to speed and continuity of long-lasting performance. It is the main ingredient to sustain personal vision and purpose. Without it, even creativity does not fuel continuous progress and love cannot maintain it.

DISCIPLINE AND CONSTANCY

Successful people have discipline and constancy. The virtue of discipline and constancy is the key to attaining greatness and achieving big results. It is the ability to focus on the right goals constantly and maintain persistence of effort.

OBJECTIVITY AND PRACTICALITY

Successful people employ objectivity and practicality in decision-making, problem-solving, planning, goal-setting and negotiating. They have a realistic approach to life. The virtue of objectivity and practicality brings the power of discrimination to achieve balanced results, which is the antidote to fanaticism.

GROUP CONSCIOUSNESS

Most successful people have a great degree of group consciousness. Group consciousness, sometimes expressed as teamwork, partially drives the business world's competitive edge and the explosive growth of corporations. This is one reason Western business currently embodies and fuels most modern definitions of success. The virtue of group consciousness is the key to sustaining power and achieving bigger goals in less time.

Let's apply the principle of success qualities by rating yourself currently and setting a development goal every six months.

KNOW YOURSELF: Rate your degree of development of the top qualities of successful people. Rate 0 to 4.	DEVELOP YOURSELF: Where would you like to be in 6 months to dramatically transform your performance? Rate 0 to 4.
Will-power and vitality _____	Will-power and vitality _____
Discipline and constancy _____	Discipline and constancy _____
Objectivity and practicality _____	Objectivity and practicality _____
Group consciousness _____	Group consciousness _____

KEYS TO TRANSFORMING SUCCESS INTO FULFILLMENT

For many who achieve external success, there is eventually a loneliness or emptiness that causes them to turn inward and start seeking fulfillment. What are the virtues or qualities necessary to transform success into fulfillment?

The keys to transform success into fulfillment become more available when a person is evolving spiritually. In a moment, we will examine how the level of a person's development affects which virtues and success components are available and being used, as well as the level of one's sense of responsibility. First, though, let's look at each key to fulfillment.

BENEVOLENCE

Fulfilled people employ benevolence. Benevolence is being loving, kind and compassionate in a selfless way. Benevolence towards others entitles you to a certain harmony and peace associated with fulfillment. The virtue of benevolence brings the power to achieve happiness, contentment and right human relations, and it is a safety key to accessing greater spiritual powers.

ALTRUISM

Fulfilled people are altruistic. Being altruistic is not just being generous at the financial or material level, but also at spiritual, mental, emotional and verbal levels in a more unconditional, unselfish way. The virtue of altruism is the key and power behind prosperity and sustained abundance. It satisfies the common expression, "What you give is what you receive back many-fold".

SACRIFICE

Fulfilled people understand and accept sacrifice as a great virtue. They act on behalf of greater good that often goes beyond the individual or family need. The virtue of sacrifice is the key to great achievements and a powerful life of service, which result in fulfillment. The virtue of sacrifice brings the power to become a legend.

GOOD HEALTH

Many fulfilled people have good health on many levels, not just physical. They are energetically, emotionally, mentally and spiritually healthy as well. The virtue of good health is the key to attaining and enjoying lasting success and fulfillment.

In the future, good health will be sought after
and valued as much as professional success.
It will be a barometer of spiritual maturity
and high culture in life.

Let's apply the principle of fulfillment qualities by rating yourself currently and setting a development goal every six months.

Know Yourself: Rate your degree of development of the top keys to transfrom success into fulfillment Rate 0 to 4.	**Develop Yourself:** Where would you like to be in 6 months to transform your success into fulfillment? Rate 0 to 4.
Benevolence ____	Benevolence ____
Altruism ____	Altruism ____
Sacrifice ____	Sacrifice ____
Good health ____	Good health ____

These virtues are discussed further in chapter 7.

As we mentioned earlier, the extent to which a person is focusing on and achieving success or fulfillment depends on their degree of development as a human being. This degree of human advancement, in turn, determines a person's level of responsibility and service. As one progresses along the path of human development as we will see in the following discussion, definitions of success and fulfillment change and evolve.

STAGES OF HUMAN DEVELOPMENT

Let's look at the progression of levels of human development.

EARLY HUMANS

Early primitive humans, due to their unevolved emotional and mental development, depended on physical instinct, stamina, vitality, strength and toughness to survive. Their power existed mostly at the physical level. They expressed the virtue of vitality to some extent. They focused on succeeding in terms of physically surviving from day to day.

AVERAGE HUMAN BEINGS

Average human beings, belonging to the masses of humanity, employ the power of emotions through lower passion, in addition to improved vitality and physical endurance. They have the constancy brought by emotional determination and passion. They are focused primarily on material success. Success is defined largely by the extent to which appetites and desires are being fed.

INTELLIGENTSIA

There are two types of intelligentsia: mental and mystical. The mental intelligentsia are more likely to be focused on material success, employing objectivity and practicality and some group consciousness to meet goals. Mystical intelligentsia define quality of life more in terms of fulfillment, expressing the virtue of sacrifice to some extent as well as a certain amount of benevolence, altruism and group consciousness.

Both the mental and mystical types of intelligentsia have started to employ not only emotional intelligence and passion, but also the power of the concrete, logical mind. Basic intuitive faculties like emotional conscience and more insightful perception are also being utilized by this group. Many intelligent professionals today belong to this level. The intelligentsia are primarily concerned with improving quality of life at individual, family and career levels.

Advanced Human Beings

Advanced human beings use their philosophical and concrete mental faculties in addition to their emotional intelligence and power of love.

They already have a sufficient development of intuitive faculties, whether they are aware of it or not. Spiritual faculties are starting to be employed as a guiding tool in their advanced work and service. Most of them, especially the mental type, are starting to integrate the power of the mind, emotions, vitality and the physical body. Advanced human beings are in the process of integrating the qualities of both success and fulfillment, and consciously or subconsciously, they are guided by a sense of service.

Saints and Sages

Saints and Sages are very advanced human beings with highly developed inner faculties who embody the three qualities of success and fulfillment, namely, will-power, love and creative intelligence. In general, Saints and Sages, especially the mental type, utilize all their physical, vitality, emotional, mental, intuitive and spiritual faculties. However, a large percentage of the mystical type of Saints and Sages still do not emphasize the physical aspects of their health due to older traditional concepts of spirituality denouncing the material aspects of life. The Saints and Sages actively and consciously apply all of the spiritual virtues and components of success and fulfillment to live a balanced life of service that contributes to the world both materially and spiritually. Many Saints and Sages are not the typical canonized ones, but rather work incognito like the Himalayan Masters.

As a person's level of development advances, so with their level of responsibility and service. Greater faculties and wisdom require greater contributions to the world to express them. As the perception of scope of responsibility and service evolves, so does the definition of success and fulfillment. The following table summarizes the level of responsibility and service for each level of human development:

LEVEL OF DEVELOPMENT	RESPONSIBILITIES AND SERVICE
Early Humans	• To oneself and immediate family
Average Human Beings	• To oneself, immediate family, relatives and friends
Intelligentsia	• To oneself, immediate family, relatives, friends, colleagues, immediate communities and social affiliations
Advanced Human Beings	• To oneself, family, relatives, friends, social affiliations, national or international projects and missions
Saints and Sages	• To humanity • To the environment and nature • To animals, plants and minerals • To Earth as a home • To other world groups working for evolution

The existing social class system like the lower, middle and upper class will soon be obsolete in grading human development. There are people from the upper class who don't serve beyond their individual needs, and some die rich without greater social contribution. Yet there are people from the lower class who rise on occasions of world need to provide great sacrifices and social contributions to humanity. Therefore, this new classification aims to categorize the degrees of human development more accurately.

KNOW YOURSELF:	DEVELOP YOURSELF:
Rate your degree of development as a human being. Check your most appropriate current level.	How developed as a human being would you like to be in 6 months? Check your desired next step or level.
Early human _____	Early human _____
Average human being _____	Average human being _____
Intelligentsia _____	Intelligentsia _____
Mental type _____	Mental type _____
Mystical type _____	Mystical type _____
Advanced human being _____	Advanced human being _____
Saint or Sage _____	Saint or Sage _____

We have discussed that there are different virtues associated with:

- Will-power
- Love
- Creative intelligence
- Success
- Fulfillment
- Levels of development

Now let's turn to some case studies to illustrate different types of people according to which qualities are more developed than others.

Case Studies of Success and Fulfillment Qualities

Case Study 1:
The Price of Ruthless Will-Power and Ambition Without Love

Arthur Manning is a politician with vision who has risen quite quickly from the ranks of local civic leader to mayor of his city. He has great ambition to be a representative in Congress in five years, and he will most likely succeed in reaching that goal. He has been smart to surround himself with very astute and experienced advisors, and he often takes their advice, but he has the reputation among them of being a dictator and is sometimes feared.

Arthur has great will-power, focus and ambition to finish whatever projects he starts, and he has proven to be resilient to the types of attacks on his reputation that are common in politics. He can stay focused on his long-term vision, and knows how to turn that pioneering vision into reality fast. He has little tolerance for slowness of action and lack of directness in communication. He values speed, and can get things done quickly.

His family life and personal relationships can be challenging. He has few real friends, although he attracts many people with his dynamic physical presence. He sometimes seems cold, indifferent and withdrawn to those closest to him because his vision is ahead of his time. He prefers not to waste time (as he sees it) socializing, except as it serves his political motives and ambitions. Long, slow, involved conversations can bore or frustrate him, and he is quick to show this boredom or frustration, especially around people he perceives to be very sentimental or "soft". Since he values a certain toughness, more emotional or loving people among his staff can seem weak to him.

Arthur is intelligent, but his main strengths rely on instincts, physical power, focus and willingness to destroy in order to create something new or obliterate any obstacle in his path, including political opponents. He has created several enemies this way.

His biggest fear is to lose his power, and this fear sometimes makes him protect his position and reputation too aggressively. He is sometimes ruthless in his actions if he feels his power is threatened. His fear makes him not hesitate to undermine the position of anyone who seems to be gaining too much power or influence compared to him.

Due to the sheer force of his will-power, Arthur's leadership and political career can last a long time, but eventually if his will-power is not balanced out by more love to preserve successful relationships, he can end up destroying his own career or those around him with the result of attracting his worst fears. Arthur definitely can't enjoy lasting peace of mind with a growing number of enemies.

QUALITIES OF SUCCESS DEVELOPED BY ARTHUR	QUALITIES OF FULFILLMENT DEVELOPED BY ARTHUR
Will-power and vitality Discipline and constancy Objectivity and practicality (partially developed)	Good health (for now)
MISSING QUALITIES	MISSING QUALITIES
Group consciousness (less developed)	Benevolence Altruism Sacrifice

Entitlement to lasting success and fulfillment as a leader – whether in politics or business – comes not just from will and force, but also must be accompanied by benevolence, altruism and harmlessness. Mahatma Gandhi had tremendous will-power, but it was his harmlessness and selflessness that enabled him to succeed against the British Empire in India without ever lifting a weapon. He demonstrated his principle of *ahimsa*, or non-violence, to fight for human rights.

SUCCESS AND FULFILLMENT STRATEGY FOR ARTHUR'S CASE:
For those who have well-developed will-power like Arthur, the next step to sustain your success and transform it into fulfillment is to develop or express more love to harmonize with others and creative intelligence to be able to employ organized plans to manifest life's goals properly.

CASE STUDY 2:
TOO MUCH LOVE WITHOUT WILL-POWER CAN HARM YOU:
The Challenges of Low Vitality and Emotionalism

Estella Walsh is a 54-year-old teacher. She loves her job because she feels that she is improving quality of life and the future of society through the children she teaches.

Estella is loved by most of her students, co-workers and supervisors. Her students often go to her for advice because she listens to them well. She has a sweet smile and magnetic personality. She has an intuitive sense for what is happening with her students and co-workers. She works effectively with others as a motivator, and can create harmony among different types of people because she has a real interest in others. Because people trust her, she tends to be a "social hub" of the school, and other teachers go to her to hear the latest news.

Whenever there is a social activity, Estella helps organize it. She remembers most people's birthdays, kids' names, favorite color and wedding anniversary. She always bakes a cake for each colleague's birthday.

While Estella is very good at inspiring her students, she becomes bored, frustrated or distracted when she has a lot of paperwork, and she doesn't perform well under tight deadlines. If she starts to feel pressured, she tends to create diversions and excuses to avoid the paperwork. She also sometimes has challenges with the math and science teachers. Even though she can usually find a way to draw them into a conversation, their introspective nature and technical language leave her feeling disconnected. She prefers not to get involved with technical discussions. She often wonders why the more technical teachers don't seem to like her or why the more ambitious teachers don't seem to have much patience with her. The friendlier she tries to be with some of them, the more they seem to withdraw from her.

When she is at her best, Estella employs both love and charisma. She is an excellent teacher and motivator because she can teach about life through stories that relate to her students. She can laser target each student's strengths and weaknesses and usually help them maximize those strengths and find effective ways to improve the weaknesses.

Estella's greatest fear is being unloved and alone. She has three additional challenges that affect her performance, success and fulfillment:

1. She doesn't care about making money. She thinks it isn't what's important in life, and she's not good at managing it. As a result, she has constant financial struggles, which create stress, fears and worry.

2. She is exhausted by the end of the day. Her fatigue is exacerbated by mild arthritis, a heart arrhythmia and sleeplessness brought on by her financial worries. Her doctors have told her that her level of exhaustion and stress could eventually result in a heart attack. Her lack of vitality causes low stress tolerance and a tendency to be pessimistic outside the classroom. She has trouble finishing what she starts beyond the structured environment of her school day and related activities.

3. She has no husband or partner in life and few close friends. She gives so much to her students and has so much grading and lesson planning to do when she goes home in the evening, she feels she has no time or energy left for a personal life. She has resigned herself to being an "old maid", which makes her sad and lonely. This is especially difficult for her since Estella's biggest fear and obstacle is to not be liked or

loved. She doesn't enjoy being alone, and her tendency to need to seek approval from others means she is over-sensitive and takes things personally.

QUALITIES OF SUCCESS DEVELOPED BY ESTELLA	QUALITIES OF FULFILLMENT DEVELOPED BY ESTELLA
Group consciousness	Benevolence Altruism (especially emotional and mental) Sacrifice
MISSING QUALITIES Will-power and vitality Discipline and constancy Objectivity and practicality	MISSING QUALITIES Good health

SUCCESS AND FULFILLMENT STRATEGY FOR ESTELLA'S CASE:

Estella's next step is to build greater vitality to overcome her fatigue, stress and poor health conditions. She needs to increase her will-power to conquer her fears and emotional limitations. To develop a proper perspective about money, she would benefit from developing more objectivity. People like her need to study chapter 4 on vitality management.

CASE STUDY 3:

A CREATIVE MIND WITHOUT A GOOD HEART CAN MAKE YOU LONELY AND UNFULFILLED

Kristina Gunther is the director of research for an international technology consortium. With a Master's degree, MBA, PhD and a double specialization in particle physics and metals, she is a highly sought-after researcher with a special talent for picking excellent technology companies to receive grants and venture funding. She has won many awards, has published many leading articles in her field and is the executive editor of an Internet-based magazine that profiles technology companies seeking funding. Her expertise is in great demand, but she still feels most comfortable in her lab. She is an eloquent speaker when addressing large meetings of her peers, but she is less comfortable if she has to speak to someone who knows nothing about particle physics, technology or start-up companies. She tends to be shy and uncomfortable at normal social events like parties.

Kristina is in constant activity, like a spider weaving a web. She is happiest when she is busy making new discoveries and contemplating new ideas. She is known around the lab and among technology funders for her mental creativity. Her peers respect and like her for her expertise and brilliance, but she has few close friends, and she isn't someone people would go to if they were in some type of emotional crisis. She often feels isolated by her advanced mental faculties even though she enjoys magnetizing her peers with her groundbreaking ideas. Many people perceive her as cold and aloof, and her need to be constantly busy and her extraordinarily quick mind alienate her from many people. She's 43 with no boyfriend and no plans to get married.

Because Kristina's mind is so quick, her humor tends to be too sharp and dry for most people, and she has a tendency to offend with her bluntness, though this is rarely her intention. She sometimes feels lonely because there aren't more people like her she can interact with and she gets tired of alienating people with her communication style. She is very conscious of global affairs and cares deeply about big social questions, but she has very little patience or regard for individuals' needs or concerns. She has little tolerance for very emotional or sentimental people and no patience with people who are slower than she is.

Kristina's greatest fear is being ignorant or "in the dark". One of her biggest obstacles is mental pride. In her mind, the worst thing she can experience is feeling stupid, not understanding something or failing. She is compulsively driven to perform, and while this gives her a certain endurance and focus, it makes her very stressed, and she affects others with her stress without being aware of it. Her mental pride isolates her from others, and sometimes she experiences a certain sadness or resentment towards more social and emotionally-skilled people who have deep, lasting relationships and circles of many friends who care about them.

QUALITIES OF SUCCESS DEVELOPED BY KRISTINA	QUALITIES OF FULFILLMENT DEVELOPED BY KRISTINA
Objectivity and practicality Discipline and constancy Will-power and vitality (partially developed)	Good health
MISSING QUALITIES Group consciousness	MISSING QUALITIES Benevolence Altruism Sacrifice

SUCCESS AND FULFILLMENT STRATEGY FOR KRISTINA'S CASE:

Developing better emotional intelligence and personality magnetism through the heart definitely would help Kristina not only be successful, but also fulfilled. Chapter 6's technique to develop the love-intellect faculty (page 155) can help people like her. Chapter 5's techniques for emotional revitalization (pages 112-115) can be studied and applied by more mental, less loving types of people.

The Secrets of Energy Anatomy for Success and Fulfillment

The universal model for success and fulfillment is not only based on the Triangle of Success and Fulfillment and the spiritual virtues, but also involves components of the human energy system. These components are shared among all people, regardless of culture, age, gender and experience. This commonality is what makes the path to success and fulfillment universal. When we understand the components of the human energy system, especially invisible components, we can have a more systematic approach to develop lasting success and fulfillment and a balanced life.

The Different Components of the Human Energy System

The four important basic components that make up a person's personality are:

1. Physical body and vitality
2. Emotions
3. Mind
4. Soul and Spirit

In order to sustain success and transform it into greater fulfillment, the principles, causes and effects triggered by these four components on one's performance, external success and internal satisfaction have to be understood. Whether it is your staying power to work, emotional magnetism, mental stamina or spiritual values, these four components are involved.

People are made up of an energy system composed of the physical body and many layers of invisible components. Let's compare a human being's system to a cellular phone to make it more tangible and concrete.

HUMAN ENERGY SYSTEM AND CELLULAR PHONE MODEL

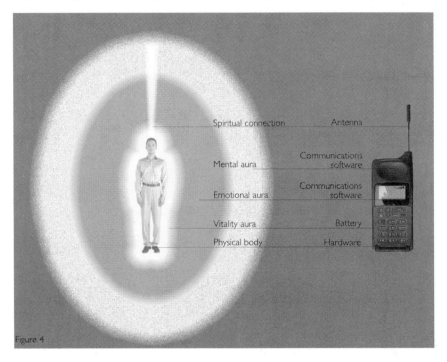

Spiritual connection   Antenna

Mental aura   Communications software

Emotional aura   Communications software

Vitality aura   Battery

Physical body   Hardware

Figure 4

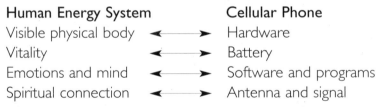

Human Energy System		Cellular Phone
Visible physical body	◄——►	Hardware
Vitality	◄——►	Battery
Emotions and mind	◄——►	Software and programs
Spiritual connection	◄——►	Antenna and signal

YOUR BODY IS YOUR HARDWARE

Your physical body has to be healthy to sustain lasting success. Poor physical health has caused many people to lose the trappings of their success. The physical component is what we see visibly as the physical body with a solid, liquid and gaseous construction. The physical body has been studied substantially by medical scientists and is recognized by almost everyone as their human self.

Visible solids vibrate at 360-750 trillion light vibrations per second. Gamma rays vibrate at approximately 3 billion billion light vibrations per second, and the vitality aura vibrates even faster, making it invisible to the normal range of eyesight

The physical part of ourselves is the grossest and lowest vibrational aspect of our bodies. When a person dies physically, the physical body gradually turns into physical earth substance, but emotional and mental energy or consciousness continue to exist for some time.

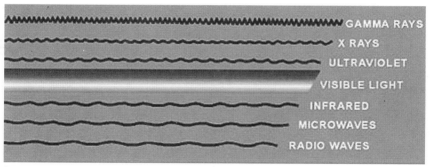

Electromagnetic spectrum: the full range of electromagnetic radiation from the longest to the shortest wavelenghts and the lowest to the highest frequencies.

Figure 5   Source: Diane Boyack, 2000

VITALITY IS YOUR LIFE'S BATTERY

In many cases, lack of vitality is what causes people to become sick, get stressed easily, deplete their will-power and switch off persistence. When a person is sick or devitalized, their talents and creativity are not optimized. Therefore, managing and sustaining your vitality is a major important component of success and fulfillment.

We all have a vitality aura, which acts like our battery. This energy is the controlling factor of vitality and stamina. If we use vitality without replenishing it, we become depleted. When vitality is constantly drained, which can be caused by stress or fatigue, it accelerates the aging process and a person can become ill.

As with different cell phone models, some people are born with a long-life battery and others are drained easily. This also depends on their emotional, mental and spiritual development. The good news is that almost everyone can charge or increase their vitality through special methods, including inner breathing, physical exercises, deep sleep, proper diet, vitamin supplements and meditation.

Our vitality aura is invisible to the naked eye, but many children or psychics can see it using their inner sight. That is, they can perceive the aura as a light around a person, even with eyes closed or not looking directly at you.

The vitality aura has many layers of refinement. The densest part is seen as the exact shape of your body, which interpenetrates and extends beyond the body a few inches for most people. It is bigger in more developed and powerful human beings. The aura of normal people is shaped like an egg with the tapered end pointing towards the bottom.

The natural energy from the air, ground, sun and food can charge the vitality body. When we do deep breathing, the oxygen revitalizes our blood and physical body because there is a component of the air called "air light globules" or air *chi* that energizes the vitality aura. The health and power of the physical body depend primarily on the vitality aura and its power centers, which we will discuss briefly in the following chapter.

You've Got an Emotional Aura:
It's the Processor of Your Feelings

Today, most successful people's determination to achieve success is fueled by their emotional passion. In addition, their emotional magnetism is what makes them great motivators and inspiring leaders. Fulfilled, happy people have the ability to emotionally attract loyal teams around them that allow their great achievement to flow and grow.

Your emotional aura is an energy field made up of the substance of your feelings, sometimes converted into your life's passion and desires. When we feel or emote, we are utilizing the emotional aura. We express positive or negative emotional attitudes because our emotions are comprised of various emotional vibrations, positive or negative.

You may have experienced effects on your emotional aura without knowing how to explain it. For example, sometimes when someone is angry at you but hasn't communicated the negative feelings towards you verbally, you can feel it, especially in the stomach area. Likewise, when you enter a very stressed office, haven't you felt your stomach knot up or get nauseous? This happens because you are feeling the negative vibration through your emotional aura, the energy aura that receives and processes feelings.

Another good example is mothers who are sensitive to the needs or problems of their children. Even at a remote distance, they can feel their children's issues or needs. Mothers can also negatively influence their children with stress. Thus stress is energetically contagious. Why? Because people are connected to their loved ones through their emotional aura, which creates "energetic osmosis".

You can purify the negative feelings of your emotional aura and recharge it with positive, pleasant emotions using special breathing and visualization techniques, which will be discussed later.

Your Mind is Your Main Software for Success

Your mind and your ability to think creatively and intelligently are two of the most important factors to bring great success and fulfillment to your life. You will learn in chapter 6 how developing your mind can make you a mental powerhouse and enable you to make a big difference.

The mind is not the brain.
The mind is the software and the brain is the hardware.

This part of our human energy anatomy is one of the most important because it differentiates us from animals. To date, most animals use only their physical and emotional instincts while humans use their minds.

The mental aura is the energy field for creating, processing, receiving and projecting thoughts. When you are thinking, which is different from feeling, you are using the energy of the mental aura. As with the emotional aura, most people have already experienced some of the faculties of the mind. Have you ever thought about what prompts you to suddenly have a strong urge to call someone like a family member or friend? When someone is thinking about you – if you are sensitive and receptive at that time – you can receive the information they are thinking or at least know that they are thinking about you and want you to call them. What's happening is telepathic rapport. It turns out that you call the person who was thinking about you or sometimes you end up calling each other simultaneously. Have you experienced this?

Your mind and emotional aura serve as the software and energetic programs that operate your entire personality, especially normal mundane activities. For more developed people, their higher aspect – called the Soul in Eastern Wisdom teachings and religions – uses the software of the mind and emotions to regulate the personality and daily life of the individual with more noble principles, inner values and faculties. The intellectual person is regulated by their mind and partially by their emotions. The average person is functioning and active at the level of the lower emotions and physical body and tends to be engrossed with excessive appetites and mediocre activities.

You can purify and recharge your mind through many methods, including inner breathing techniques, affirmations, visualization and continuous study. By using the faculties of the mind constantly, it is being exercised to develop mental powers and stamina. When the mind is not used for a long period or stretched regularly with bigger ideas and new concepts, it starts to crystallize and atrophy. This can partially cause Parkinson's disease and Alzheimer's. In a comatose person, the mind is disconnected from the brain. The mind – as distinct from the brain – will be a subject of new research and study in the coming generation. More technical details about the mind and how it works will be discussed in chapter 6.

YOUR SPIRITUAL ANTENNA IS A PATHWAY OF INSPIRATION AND INTUITION

The antenna signal of the cell phone affects how useful the communication equipment is. It's the same for you. Even with a good mind, stable emotions and a strong physical body, there can be absence of inspiration experienced as deep loneliness or apathy when your spiritual antenna is weak or has bad reception. Your wisdom and intuition can be developed by improving your "spiritual signal".

Many top successful executives and political leaders have expressed to me that they feel deep emptiness despite having accomplished most of their goals successfully. The spiritual connection that provides the greater purpose of one's life to move to the next great step is what's missing for some of these successful leaders. And sometimes their Soul's will and purpose run contrary to these leaders' decisions or normal reasoning. I have found that techniques like meditation, coaching sessions and deeper inner reflection guided by an experienced spiritual mentor will help process a few obstructing misconceptions about what is important in their lives. Usually after several sessions, the client's spiritual connections start opening, and the person becomes greatly inspired.

As a result, many of my clients and seminar participants are able to connect to their spirituality, simplify their lifestyle and use some of their financial and material resources to create or support non-profit organizations and charities meeting world needs. As soon as they are spiritually-motivated, these successful leaders become better agents of global transformation and experience greater fulfillment.

Many wealthy businesspeople and successful professionals in India and Asia, and now starting in Europe and America, leave their families, businesses and careers in search of spiritual inspiration and the unfoldment of advanced human faculties to make the next great leap in their lives. Greatness normally demands great sacrifice, selflessness and total surrender to higher inspiration. In my own quest trekking in the Himalayan Mountains, I met renunciates dressed like beggars with long beards and sandals who used to be very successful and wealthy executives from Europe, North and South America and Australia. When I asked them why they left their homes and sacrificed their material and social life and families, their answers were all similar: to search for a different, fuller meaning of life and existence.

I believe that we do not have to drop everything, including our past achievements and loved ones, in this search. A spiritual science like the strategies offered in this book provides modern techniques to discover the light of fuller existence and service to achieve self-fulfillment without abandoning our normal lives. We can flower where we are planted.

KNOW YOURSELF: Rate the level of development of your physical and energy anatomy components. Rate 0 to 4.	DEVELOP YOURSELF: Where would you like to be for your next step in 6 months? Rate 0 to 4.
Physical body ____	Physical body ____
Vitality ____	Vitality ____
Emotions ____	Emotions ____
Spiritual antenna/ inspiration ____	Spiritual antenna/ inspiration ____

The rest of this book discusses each of the components of the Success and Fulfillment Triangle and the human energy system in separate chapters and provides practical techniques to boost performance for greater success and fulfillment. Before we turn to the different components, though, we need to study and understand the energy anatomy called the "human power centers", often called the "chakras" in spiritual literature.

My spiritual mentors have given priceless information about the secrets of the power centers through their advanced perspective, especially MCKS, one of the world's greatest healers, who has revealed the modern science of the chakras. I have also included many of my personal experiences as a martial arts master, healing expert and a teacher of the Eastern Wisdom philosophy.

Let's turn to the next chapter to reveal the secrets of the human power centers.

CHAPTER 3

THE SECRETS OF YOUR POWER CENTERS REVEALED

◆

A key ingredient in achieving what you want and enjoying what you have is understanding how your energy affects your performance. The level of your available will-power, love and creative intelligence depends on your "energy anatomy" and its power centers. These power centers are known in Eastern traditions like martial arts, healing sciences and yoga as "chakras", and the development of the power centers is a main goal of advanced meditation and many breathing techniques. Let's explore how the secrets of your power centers can give you a valuable edge in your professional and personal life.

YOUR POWER CENTERS OR CHAKRAS:
Seats of Aptitude, Attitude and Virtue Development

The condition of your energy and vitality is a predictor of success, and it is affected by the quality and activity of your power centers. Even your ability to think creatively, feel happy and be inspired is all a function of the degree of your power centers' awakening.

The training of the Himalayan Masters involves daily stimulation of these hidden energy centers through breathing techniques, sacred sound chants and meditation. Many of these techniques are revealed in this book.

The power centers are familiar to most yoga practitioners and martial artists and are a central component of the Eastern Wisdom teachings.

Yoga practitioners activate these energy centers to expand spiritual experience and to develop faculties like compassion, inner peace, awareness, will-power, focus, creativity, intuition, wisdom and inspiration. Martial artists focus on certain power centers to develop physical instincts, reflexes, resilience, vitality, stamina and will-power.

To maximize overall performance, success and fulfillment, you will be activating certain power centers through concentration and breathing methods. This book offers non-traditional approaches to cultivating a totally successful life, but even more, a balanced, fulfilled existence. These methods are not yet familiar to most Western executives as of today, but they are to many Eastern professionals and spiritual seekers in places like India, Korea, Japan, Indonesia, China, Russia and the Philippines.

Let's define what power centers are and how they function.

FUNCTIONS AND DESCRIPTIONS OF THE POWER CENTERS

1. Power centers act like switches or keys to access inner faculties, spiritual powers and virtues like those we have discussed in the earlier chapter: will-power, vitality, discipline and constancy, love, benevolence, altruism, creative intelligence, objectivity and practicality, group consciousness, sacrifice and good health.
2. Some energy centers are utilized by the Soul or spiritual consciousness to control certain physiological and psychological functions, including what we call good and bad situations in life like diseases.
3. These power centers regulate vitality, emotional attitudes and mental aptitudes. These faculties are tabulated on pages 67-69.

4. These invisible vortices of vibrations and forces serve as transmitters of energy and information within, into and out of the auras.
5. The energy centers act like energy software and subconscious programs for the proper functioning of the body's organs and systems, thus controlling health.

You have many power centers in your body that you can energetically switch on to stimulate your human faculties, aptitudes, attitudes or virtues gradually or rapidly.

When the power centers are more developed, they are seen by trained clairvoyants or psychics to have brighter light, higher-speed rotation and a bigger diameter. The complete energy construction of the power centers and their advanced inner powers are discussed in detail in my book, *Inner Powers to Maximize Your Performance*. For the techniques you will use in this book, the locations of the important power centers involved are illustrated on the next page.

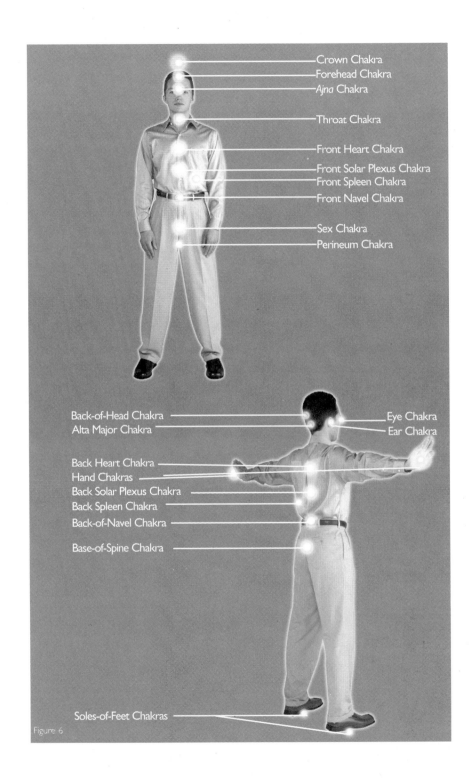

Crown Chakra
Forehead Chakra
Ajna Chakra

Throat Chakra

Front Heart Chakra

Front Solar Plexus Chakra
Front Spleen Chakra
Front Navel Chakra

Sex Chakra
Perineum Chakra

Back-of-Head Chakra
Alta Major Chakra

Eye Chakra
Ear Chakra

Back Heart Chakra
Hand Chakras
Back Solar Plexus Chakra
Back Spleen Chakra
Back-of-Navel Chakra

Base-of-Spine Chakra

Soles-of-Feet Chakras

Figure 6

Let's discuss each power center briefly.

TOP-OF-HEAD OR CROWN POWER CENTER

This center is located at the top of the head. When this center is highly stimulated or activated – especially regularly for a long time – it harnesses the powers of intuition, unconditional love and wisdom, and it brings inspiration down from the Soul. It is one of the most important power centers to understand, activate and empower for spiritual faculties and higher faculty development. This energy center stimulates the virtues of benevolence, altruism, sacrifice and group consciousness on a global scale. It is very developed in Sages, Saints and world servers.

The cone shape on the head of the Buddha, which symbolizes full illumination and wisdom with a complete set of 1,000 all-seeing eyes equivalent to complete enlightenment. The Buddha is the embodiment of full wisdom and enlightenment.

The crown of Jesus the Christ with 12 stars and points. When seen with inner sight, this power center has 12 golden petal-like energies and, when fully developed, 12 opened petals like a crown or open lotus flower. The Catholic symbol of holiness and spiritual leadership is a miter worn on the head by the Pope and bishops. This crown symbol is also embodied in the three kings of Christianity who visited Jesus the Christ when he incarnated in Bethlehem.

The Shaman's many-feathered headdress, which symbolizes spiritual leadership as the tribal head.

The crown and halo of saints and Christian angels, which is the artist's portrayal of the crown center

Figure 7

FOREHEAD POWER CENTER

This power center is located at the forehead area and is responsible for the faculties of memory, intuitional insightfulness and greater awareness. It is a hidden energy center that most yogis and healers do not know about. It is also not usually known among most meditators and spiritual teachers. Emotional excitement and the ability to sense pleasure, including orgasm, are also regulated by this power center, which controls the pleasure and pain center of the brain, the limbic system. Mystics and psychics have more active forehead power centers than scientists or concrete-minded people.

MID-BROW OR AJNA POWER CENTER

This power center is between the eyebrows. It is symbolized externally in some cultures: for example, Indian women with a red dot between the eyebrows and the headdress of Egyptian pharoahs with a cobra and vulture head in the mid-brow area representing their more developed *ajna* power center. Most yogis, healers and internal martial artists emphasize stimulating this point for mental will-power and abstract mental intelligence.

Have you observed that when you need to push heavy objects or increase your lifting power, you squint your mid-brow naturally? This tends to boost your will-power. Also, when you concentrate on a deep thought or try to solve a complicated problem, you tend to furrow or squint this area, which increases your ability to focus. If you observe willful people, they have more wrinkles on the forehead and between the eyes because of the habit of squinting when increasing their forcefulness.

Great leaders usually employ great will-power, mental stamina, vision and abstract thinking because they are endowed with or have developed this mid-brow power center. To develop the virtue of discipline and constancy, this power center must be active.

THROAT POWER CENTER

The throat power center is located at the center of the throat. It is closely associated with objectivity and practicality and is the center for the expression of the concrete mind. It is also related to concrete intelligence and discrimination. A well-developed throat power center is necessary to transform ideas into plans, organized activity and results. If this power center is over-developed without the heart, the person becomes over-critical and too meticulous.

Many scientists, accountants, lawyers and businesspeople have more developed throat power centers than mystics and loving type people.

HEART POWER CENTER

The center of power probably most familiar to people is the heart, which is related to emotional intelligence, charisma and the love nature. The ability to love and be loved by people is one of the most powerful instruments to sustain leadership and influence. The faculties of love, compassion, altruism and benevolence utilize the heart center, especially guided by the unconditional love nature stimulated by the top-of-head center. This is commonly depicted in portraits of religious Saints as the brightness and beam of golden light emanating from the center of their chest.

When we fall in love or do good things for others, we feel a pleasurable, warm sensation in our chest area. Likewise, when a person violates the heart's virtues against others, the chest feels heavy, constricted and closed. This center of love expands or contracts depending on the activity and emotion projected or received by the individual. By activating this power center, you can feel love, peace and happiness, and the ability to forgive others becomes natural. Mystics and saintly people are naturally endowed with a big, active heart center, thus they are emotionally sensitive.

Many scientists, technically-minded people and business executives need to develop this center more so that their heart centers are as developed and active as their minds. Businesspeople who are turning to philanthropic work are already opening their hearts. It is one of the keys to happiness and enjoying what you have in life.

SOLAR PLEXUS POWER CENTER

This energy center is located at the center of the abdominal area just below the sternum. This power center is the seat of passion, desire and lower emotions – both positive and negative. The solar plexus usually accumulates stress, fear, anger, nervousness and guilty feelings. That is why people experience pressure or a burning sensation in the solar plexus area when they are in a negative state.

This center is so important because it stimulates the energy for courage, commitment and determination, three qualities that very successful people have developed.

When this center is over-stimulated, the person becomes unstable and emotionally reactive, sometimes leading to abrasiveness and stress. In most people, this power center should be regulated because its energy also exacerbates greed and self-centeredness, which work against the qualities needed to attain life's fulfillment. A well-developed, active heart can transform the negative impact of the solar plexus center.

NAVEL POWER CENTER

This power center is used most by the Himalayan Masters, martial arts masters and advanced yogis in their inner practices and meditation. By breathing slowly and focusing on this power center, you can improve the following:

- Internal power for stamina and the body's rejuvenation
- Absorption, assimilation and circulation of internal vitality as a reserve of power
- Speed, instinct and agility in your physical reactions and movements
- Good gut instincts and timing in decision-making
- Sexual potency

This energy center is weak and underdeveloped in many people who are easily devitalized or sexually impotent, move slowly or have poor timing in decision-making.

The degree of navel power center development separates the

super-athlete from the ordinary. If you look at the best golfers and basketball players clairvoyantly, they share one thing in common: Their navel power centers are more active and developed than in most players.

The faculties of the navel center apply in the business world as well. When a trained clairvoyant or good psychic examines the energy and auras of the best business decision-makers and great leaders, they can see that the navel power centers are bigger, brighter and more developed than their subordinates' or peers'.

Why then do these good decision-makers sometimes commit serious mistakes? Because there are different degrees of penetrating truth, and the navel center instinct is just one of them. Sometimes higher mental discrimination is needed to override instinctive knowing. These higher faculties are developed from the top-of-head, forehead, mid-brow, throat and heart centers.

Not only is the development of the navel power center important, so is the amount of energy stored in it. When the vitality of the navel power center is low, instincts are off. Therefore, there is a need to constantly activate and energize the navel power center. I have experimented with activating and energizing the navel power center of athletes, and I have found that it definitely improves their performance immediately. In the future, internal energy employing the navel center will catch the attention of Olympic and professional athletes to break records easily in their chosen sports. I also use navel center breathing techniques with our offsite retreat groups. As a result, they don't need to acclimatize during mountain climbs because we boost internal strength and stamina through the breathing methods to improve mileage dramatically, especially at high altitude.

I also teach these techniques to sexually impotent clients and after several weeks, their problems are solved. And imagine if this navel breathing were taught to astronauts: I believe their health would improve and the negative side effects of anti-gravity such as muscular or skeletal deterioration would be minimized.

Simple methods involving activating the navel center's power will be discussed in the next chapters.

SPLEEN POWER CENTER

This center is a generator of vitality and helps the body purify toxins. It is very important for maintaining good health. It is located below the floating ribcage to the left of the stomach area. When this energy center is weak, people are usually depressed and affected by poor weather conditions, especially when there is minimal exposure to the sun. The spleen center definitely has to be active and healthy to sustain a high output of work and great staying power. Again, as we mentioned earlier, the power centers or chakras affect our health – physically, psychologically and spiritually. With low vitality and poor health, all the other human faculties don't function properly, and success and fulfillment are just a dream.

SEX POWER CENTER

This center is located in front of the pubic area and reproductive organs and is responsible for sexual vitality, procreativity and, indirectly, creativity. There is a direct relationship between sexual energy, creativity and success. Creative people are usually sexual in nature, and they tend to be smarter, innovative and artistic. A well-developed sense of humor is also an expression of creativity and is connected to sexual energy.

Personal magnetism can be enhanced by the power of the sex center, along with the magnetic energy of the heart. This is normally called "sex appeal". In many instances, success and fulfillment are connected to personal charisma and a magnetic presence that enhance motivational leadership and power of influence.

There is a technique to use the energy of the sex center to energize the brain and the mind to prevent senile decay that comes with age.

Wouldn't it be nice to grow very old, still sexually appealing and mentally brilliant until our last breath?

BASE-OF-SPINE POWER CENTER

The base-of-spine power center is located in the coccyx area at the base of the spine. It governs the basic will to survive and the ability to materialize goals. Wealthy and powerful people have well-developed and strong base-of-spine power centers. This power center is also associated with the strength and health of the hips, legs, knees, feet, muscles and bones. The base-of-spine center is necessary for a grounded, practical approach to life that balances spiritual fulfillment with material success.

POWER CENTERS:
Keys to Success and Fulfillment

POWER CENTERS	LOCATION	FUNCTIONS, APTITUDES, ATTITUDES AND VIRTUES THEY ACTIVATE
Crown	Top of head (center)	• Unconditional love, inclusiveness, benevolence, altruism, virtue of sacrifice and detachment • Global consciousness • Intuition, spiritual vision, wisdom, serenity, bliss and inspiration
Forehead	Center of forehead	• Insightfulness, spiritual vision, awareness • Emotional sensitivity to pleasure and pain • Memory and imaginativeness
Mid-Brow or *Ajna*	Between eyebrows	• Abstract and principle-based thinking and philosophical mental aptitudes • Capacity to mentally understand and creativity through higher ideas • Mental stamina and will-power, ability to focus and be one-pointed • Virtue of discipline and constancy

Power Centers	Location	Functions, Aptitudes, Attitudes and Virtues they Activate
Throat	Middle of throat	• Concrete and critical thinking, capacity for details • Communication skills and accurate mental perception • Virtue of objectivity and practicality
Heart	Mid-chest	• Personal love nature, compassion, emotional intelligence, joy and inner peace • Virtues of benevolence, altruism, sacrifice and group consciousness • Emotional magnetism and power to inspire • Ability to attract successful relationships
Solar Plexus	Center of abdomen below sternum	• Courage, emotional commitment and determination • Passion and desire (both positive and negative) • Happiness
Spleen	Left side of abdomen below the floating ribcage	• Vitality and good health • Purification of toxins
Navel	Navel or belly button	• Instincts, agility, timing and guts in decision-making • Vitality and internal energy/stamina • Rejuvenation

POWER CENTERS	LOCATION	FUNCTIONS, APTITUDES, ATTITUDES AND VIRTUES THEY ACTIVATE
Sex	In front of pubic area and repro-ductive organs	• Sexual appeal and personal magnetism • Energy fuel for creativity, artistic ability, sense of humor and spiritual growth • Happiness through fulfilling sexual relationship
Base-of-Spine	Base of spine at the coccyx	• Practical instincts, especially for financial and material results • Physical health and stamina • Ability to materialize goals

To illustrate functions, aptitudes, attitudes and virtues activated by the power centers, let's look at the comparative case study below of world leaders and executives. Trained clairvoyants have determined the activity level of the power centers of these great leaders and executives.

LEADERS OR EXECUTIVES	POWER CENTERS THAT ARE VERY ACTIVE AND MORE DEVELOPED
Mother Teresa (before she died)	Top-of-head, forehead, heart, solar plexus
Mahatma Gandhi (before he died)	Top-of-head, forehead, mid-brow, heart, solar plexus, spleen, navel
Martin Luther King, Jr. (before he died)	Top-of-head, throat, heart, solar plexus, sex
Winston Churchill (before he died)	Mid-brow, throat, solar plexus, navel
Bill Gates (Microsoft CEO) (On December 15, 2003)	Top-of-head, mid-brow, throat, heart, solar plexus, spleen, navel, sex, base-of-spine

Leaders or Executives	Power Centers that are Very Active and More Developed
Jack Welch (Former CEO, GE) (On December 15, 2003)	Mid-brow, throat, solar plexus, navel, sex, base-of-spine
Steve Jobs (CEO, Apple) (On December 15, 2003)	Top-of-head, forehead, mid-brow, throat, heart, solar plexus, spleen, sex, base-of-spine
Bill Clinton (Former US President) (On December 15, 2003)	Throat, heart, solar plexus, navel, sex
George W. Bush, Jr. (US President) (On December 15, 2003)	Mid-brow, throat, heart, solar plexus, base-of-spine
Mikhail Gorbachev (Former President of The Soviet Union) (On December 15, 2003)	Mid-brow, throat, heart, solar plexus

Note: This tabulation does not reflect the development of the above leaders and executives compared to each other, but rather demonstrates the comparison of the different power centers within the person's own development, triggering balance or imbalance. The more power centers that are active, the more balanced the individual, especially involving the upper and lower centers. The spiritual power center, the top-of-head, should match the size of the base-of-spine material power center for a balanced material and spiritual life.

THE CENTERS THAT TRIGGER SUCCESS AND FULFILLMENT ARE AS FOLLOWS:

MATERIAL AND CAREER SUCCESS:	Mid-brow, throat, solar plexus, navel, sex and base-of-spine centers
INNER FULFILLMENT:	Top-of-head, forehead, heart, navel, sex and base-of-spine centers

The future approach and psychology for both material success and spiritual fulfillment will inevitably employ the new science of the power centers. This criterion will be included in hiring personnel, identifying the right leaders for the job and matching workers and responsibilities.

The matrix of success and fulfillment will be deliberately sculptured and shaped by the application of Eastern Wisdom methods and spiritual science. Most principles and techniques for success still focus on university schooling, job-related leadership and executive training and the slow and arduous path of trial and error. Many failures usually delay the process in this traditional approach to success.

This slow approach will change in the future by using the stimulation of the energy anatomy and power centers to hone more advanced and balanced human faculties and virtues. This will be a major subject for training people to maximize their potential and achievement.

You don't have to wait for the future to arrive, though. You can have an edge now, today, by applying your new understanding of your own energy anatomy and power centers to further develop and apply your will-power, love and creative intelligence for integrated power.

The rest of this book will help you do this systematically. Let's proceed to learn how the secrets of the Himalayan Masters can make your life happier, healthier and more fulfilled.

CHAPTER 4

YOU CAN DEVELOP YOUR WILL-POWER AND VITALITY FAST

◆

Why is vitality critical to success and fulfillment? Because it is a key ingredient in one of the three major components in the Success and Fulfillment Triangle: will-power. Without will-power, success is hard to achieve and maintain, and fulfillment is difficult to imagine. Love and creative intelligence are not enough for total success and fulfillment.

Vitality and will-power are the 4-wheel drive to take you up the mountains of life. They help you materialize goals. They help make abstract ideas concrete realities. They give you the power to finish what you start faster.

Without will-power, obstacles seem bigger than they are, optimism is hard to maintain, it's harder to focus on solutions rather than problems and there is less stress tolerance, as we saw with Estella Walsh, our teacher case study. Will-power cannot exist without high levels of sustained vitality. Vitality is one of the key shared qualities of super-achievers.

Have you ever experienced waking up in the morning feeling that you are too weak or old to tackle important work or start new projects? Or sometimes it feels as if your life has lost its power, and that it won't last long? Why does this happen?

It has to do with vitality and will-power. If your vitality is low, you are like a cell phone or car with a dead battery. No matter how intelligent, determined or enthusiastic you are, when your energy and will-power are down, you cannot function properly. Vitality is like the gasoline energizing success and fueling accomplishments. Without it, our talent and ambitions don't work. Many great successful people are prone to fail when vitality is drained.

Vitality levels also affect mental and emotional aptitude and attitude. One of the single most important factors for staying on top of your life and achieving your goals is the ability to maintain constant vitality. People with higher vitality have better health, make better decisions, solve problems more effectively, have more negotiating power and enjoy quality relationships.

Maximizing your performance depends largely on the will-power to overcome your stress and critical difficulties in life. Even your ability to overcome fears, depression and diseases depends on the ability to apply will-power, which depends on maintaining vitality. For this reason, an entire chapter of this book addresses vitality development and management.

KNOW YOURSELF:
Assess your current level of vitality by answering the following questions.

	Yes	No
I feel tired most of the time.		
By the end of the day, I feel low on energy.		
I get stressed or irritated easily.		
Sometimes I feel too old to start new things.		
I have trouble finishing what I start.		

If you answered "yes" to more than one of these questions, you may need to develop more vitality and will-power using our 8-step technique, which is discussed in this chapter.

8-Step Exercise to Boost Vitality Fast

One of the foundations of managing stress and maintaining high vitality is Internal Stamina Exercise™, a 5- to 10-minute series of effective exercises synchronized with breathing techniques.

I used to exercise two hours a day to stay fit for competition during my martial arts competition days. I employed physical training power more than internal power. But as I learned the secrets of internal energy through my healing mastery, I combined both of these above methods and designed a quick and effective way of purifying, revitalizing and balancing the human energy system. Five to 10 minutes of this method give more internal energy and balance than my normal one-hour athletic and martial arts training.

In maintaining stamina, it is important to increase the energy level by circulating oxygenated blood in the whole body for fast rejuvenation. To sustain internal stamina, energy should be distributed throughout the human energy system properly. You don't have to over-exert your body to accumulate energy faster and build stamina.

Internal Stamina Exercise:
You Can Do It Anywhere, Anytime... With No Special Gadgets!

The Internal Stamina Exercise program was designed with these expected benefits:

- Rejuvenate the body and release stress and body tension
- More oxygen in the blood and the body to enhance metabolism, accelerate weight loss and purify and detoxify the whole body
- Improve body strength and stamina without getting tired
- Increase vitality and improve its proper circulation throughout the entire body
- Release toxins and stress from all the internal organs and aura

Specially-designed for today's busy professionals, this method does not require special equipment or accessories and can be done almost anywhere, anytime. You can do the exercises and breathing techniques in a business suit in your office, at a conference or during work breaks. A DVD video version, Beat Your Fatigue and Stress Fast (available online at www.mdpglobal.com), demonstrates and explains all the techniques, but let's discuss the details here as well.

I recommend that you try these exercises before proceeding to the rest of this book. The entire Internal Stamina Exercise program is described in the following pages, including step-by-step photographs of how to do each exercise. The key is the full breathing along with the physical movement!

8-Step Internal Stamina Exercise:
EXERCISES WITH SYNCHRONIZED BREATHING TECHNIQUES
(see Figure 8, pages 80-86)

PREPARATION

1. You may follow the DVD video guiding this program.
2. You can achieve best results with a clean fresh air supply or ventilation in your exercise space. Once you have familiarized yourself with the sequence, do it outdoors, if possible.

PROCEDURE

1. SHOULDER AND SPINE STRESS RELEASE (10 times): to release tension in your abdominal area, upper body and spine (see page 80)
   - Place your hands together in front of your navel.
   - Inhale fully and rapidly as you pull your bent arms towards the back with your head tilted backwards (as though you were looking at the sky) and your back arched.
   - Exhale fully and rapidly as you curl yourself forward, chin in, and simultaneously bring your hands back to the front at navel level.

2. **ARM SWING** (10 times): to oxygenate your lungs and blood and empower your upper torso (see page 81)
    * Extend your arms together in front of your chest.
    * Inhale fully as you swing your arms around your shoulders by circling them up backwards.
    * Exhale fully as you bring them back down to the front.

3. **UPPER BODY TURNS** (10 times in each direction): to release tension in your upper torso and spine and to balance the left and right sides of your body (see page 82)
    * Place your feet at shoulder width.
    * Join your knuckles in front of your chest.
    * Inhale fully as you turn to the far right and exhale as you swing back to the far left 10 times, then reverse direction.

4. **HIP ROLLS** (10 times in each direction): to loosen up your hips and flow vitality throughout your body (see page 83)
    * Put your hands on your hips.
    * Rotate your hips to the right in a circular motion 10 times.
    * Then reverse direction 10 times.

5. **INTERNAL ORGANS EXERCISE** (10 times): to detoxify, revitalize and exercise your internal organs (not recommended for people with internal organ problems and pregnant women) (see page 84)
    * Place your feet at shoulder width and bend your knees slightly.
    * Inhale fully and rapidly while expanding your abdomen.
    * Exhale fully and rapidly while compressing your abdomen.
    * Continue rapid and full inhalations and exhalations.

6. **EXPANDING SQUATS** (20-30 times): for anti-aging, increased will-power and to enhance blood and vitality circulation throughout your body (not recommended for people with knee problems) (see page 84)
    * Place your feet at shoulder width.
    * Put your palms together at the center of your chest with fingers pointing upwards.
    * Inhale fully.
    * Exhale fully as you squat down, bending your knees and expanding your arms fully stretched to the side.
    * Inhale fully as you come up, bringing your palms back to the center position.
       After doing all the squats, stand steadily while concentrating on the top of your head and soles of your feet simultaneously. Breathe slowly and relax for 30 seconds. This technique facilitates the flow of vitality and power in your entire body.

7. **WHOLE BODY STRETCH** (10 times): to align your entire body, release the pressure on your spine and strengthen your lower legs and feet (see page 85)
    * Place your feet together.
    * Put your palms together at the center of your chest with your fingers pointing upwards.
    * Inhale fully as you pull your hands as high as you can over the top of your head, stretching your whole body on tip-toe.
    * Exhale fully as you return to the starting position with your hands back at chest level.

8. **SIDE-TO-SIDE BODY STRETCH** (10 times): to loosen up the sides of your body and further oxygenate your lungs and blood (see page 86)
    * Place your feet at shoulder width.
    * Put your palms together at the center of your chest with your fingers pointing upwards.
    * Inhale fully as you pull your hands over your head as high as you can.

- While holding your breath, tilt your upper body to the right, then to the left and back to the center starting position.
- Exhale as you bring your hands down to the original position at chest level.

INTERNAL STAMINA EXERCISE SCHEDULE

The Internal Stamina Exercise is recommended at least three times a week or, even better, daily before and after work. You can do it after your morning shower before you go to work for more energy throughout the whole day. It is also helpful after a stressful day to revitalize yourself before spending time with your family. I do this exercise after a long flight to successfully beat flight fatigue. You can try experimenting with the program for one week to observe how you feel compared to days you don't do it.

Internal Stamina Exercise
SHOULDER AND SPINE STRESS RELEASE (10 TIMES)

Starting position

Exhale rapidly as you curl yourself foward, chin in and bring your hands to the front.

Inhale rapidly as you pull your arms towards the back with your head tilted backwards and your back arched.

Ending position

Figure 8-1

ARM SWING   (10 TIMES)

Inhale fully as you swing your arms around your shoulders by circling them up backwards.

Exhale fully as you bring them back to the front.

Starting position

Ending position

Figure 8-2

UPPER BODY TURNS   (10 TIMES IN EACH DIRECTION)

Repeat in the opposite
direction for another
10 sets.

Exhale fully as you swing to
the left. Do this 10 times.

Inhale fully as you twist
to the right.

Starting position

Figure 8-3

HIP ROLLS   (10 Times in each direction)

Starting position

Rotate your hips to the right
in a circular motion 10 times.

Then to the left 10 times

Figure 8-4

INTERNAL ORGANS EXERCISE   (10 TIMES)

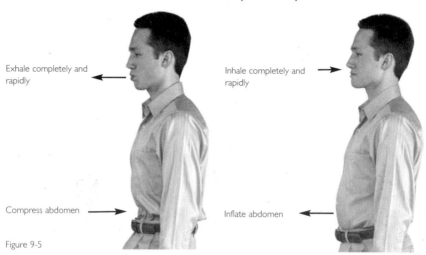

Exhale completely and rapidly

Inhale completely and rapidly

Compress abdomen

Inflate abdomen

Figure 9-5

EXPANDING SQUATS   (20-30 TIMES)

Inhale fully in the starting position.

Then exhale completely as you squat down.

Inhale fully as you return to the starting position.

Starting position
Figure 8-6

Squatting position

Keep back straight

WHOLE BODY STRETCH   (10 TIMES)

Starting position

Inhale fully as you stretch your whole body with your hands up as high as you can, on tip-toe.

Exhale completely as you return to the starting position.

Figure 8-7

SIDE-TO-SIDE BODY STRETCH   (10 TIMES)

Inhale fully as you stretch your hands over your head.

Hold your breath and stretch from side to side.

Starting position

Exhale completely as you return to the starting position.

Figure 8-8

THE SCIENCE OF BREATHING
For Internal Stamina Development

Now that you have done the 8-step Internal Stamina Exercise, you have experienced the power and effectiveness that come from the synchronization of the breathing with the exercise.

Let's explore the importance of the science of breathing further and learn some breathing techniques that can help boost your vitality for better performance.

Why is the science of breathing so important? Breath is life. People can go without food or drink for a few days or a week, and they can go without sunlight for a month. But most people can't go more than a few minutes without air. Why? Because we cannot survive in the absence of oxygen. Not only that: the vitality and energy that vivify and revitalize your physical body, with all its systems and organs, and your vitality aura depend on the energy that comes from the air, which we can call "air vitality", "air *prana*" in yoga or "*chi*" in martial arts.

HOW THE BODY USES OXYGEN
Let's examine how the body uses oxygen:

- Oxygen is needed for the proper transformation of food nutrients into energy harnessed by the cells in the internal metabolic process. The ability to convert food into energy makes the food we eat valuable. People can eat healthy food, but an inadequate level of oxygen in the conversion process, as well as other factors like iron deficiency, can lead to low vitality and malnutrition.
- Oxygen and air vitality absorbed properly through the lungs by full breathing techniques enable the blood to displace the toxins in the body effectively, especially carbon dioxide. Also, the absorbed air vitality is distributed to the power centers and the aura, resulting in rapid revitalization.
- Rapid breathing techniques energize and empower the nervous system through the absorption of ions via nerves in the

internal nasal cavity. Therefore, certain rapid breathing techniques can be employed to facilitate this process.

BREATHING AND BODY POSTURE

Since breathing techniques are especially effective methods to energize the body rapidly, let's discuss the significance of breathing patterns for health and vitality. Posture is one of the most important
factors impacting the effectiveness of the breathing process.

Proper body posture not only determines air intake capacity, but
also one's mental, emotional and spiritual aspects. Observe and
consider the ways different people sit and breathe:

- *Alert and smarter people* generally sit upright most of the time,
  especially when they are thinking or doing their most important work. They have better breathing habits, except when
  they get stressed; then breathing becomes more shallow and
  erratic.
- *Depressed people and pessimists* have a concave, curled body
  posture when sitting or sleeping. This creates a compressed
  diaphragm, reduced lung capacity and restricted oxygen intake,
  resulting in low vitality and reduced power.
- *Stressed people and people with anxiety* generally breathe
  through chest movement and expansion while the abdomen
  is held tucked in, accompanied by a shallow and erratic breathing pattern. Again, less air intake means less oxygen and air
  energy, resulting in poorer health. If this type of person has
  been exposed to severe stress and anxiety for an extended
  period, they develop the pattern of shallow breathing, even
  while resting or relaxing.

  Proper healthy breathing involves abdominal movement and
  expansion to draw more air deeper into the lower lobes of
  the lungs, which results in the abdomen expanding, not the
  chest.
- *Insecure and defensive people* usually sit with crossed legs and
  arms. The closed position does not allow them to absorb vital-

ity from the environment or from the power of ideas during a lecture or conversation. People in this position are not in a receptive mood, so it's best not to present your ideas and recommendations until they uncross their arms and legs. Students who sit in this position while listening to the teacher do not absorb as much information. Do not continue negotiating or trying to give advice to your business clients, colleagues or even to your children when they are standing or sitting with arms and/or legs crossed.

However, this position can be useful on occasion: Crossing the arms and legs is an immediate shielding technique when you are with very negative and stressed people or are in a negatively charged environment.

Know Yourself:
What does your posture and breathing style say about you? Identify your type.

Alert type with upright posture   _____

Lazy with laid back, reclining position   _____

Pessimistic and worrying type with
drooped shoulders and concave chest   _____

Stressed and anxious type with chest
breathing and no abdominal expansion   _____

Insecure or defensive type with frequently
crossed arms and/or legs   _____

EXPERIMENT WITH THIS CONCEPT:

- *Businesspeople*: Test the receptiveness of clients sitting in the defensive position.
- *School teachers*: Observe the students who do well and those who under-perform. How do they sit?
- *Healthcare professionals and healers:* How do sickly patients sit compared to healthier people?
- *Coaches or team leaders:* How do high achievers sit compared to pessimists or lower performers?
- *Business leaders:* How do your best employees sit compared to under-performers? How do your stressed and unhealthy employees breathe? Observe the abdomen and chest.
- *Parents:* Observe how your children sit. Who is healthier and more active?

Wrong body posture can create negative physical, emotional and mental health and attitudes, or vice-versa. By positioning the body properly while sitting, standing or sleeping, plus breathing properly by inhaling deeply into the abdomen instead of the chest, greater health and substantial internal power and energy result. The physical exercises and meditations presented in this book always include breathing techniques.

BREATHING PATTERNS

Most people exhibit several breathing patterns such as:

- Abdominal breathing
- Chest breathing
- Shoulder breathing

Different breathing patterns are formed depending on health, stress level and consciousness.

ABDOMINAL BREATHING

This natural method involves expanding the abdomen during inhalation and deflating the abdomen during exhalation. Observe the natural breathing of a healthy sleeping baby. The belly expands during inhalation and deflates during exhalation.

CHEST BREATHING

Highly stressed people usually breathe with more chest expansion and minimal abdominal movement. When people have anxiety, anger or high levels of emotional tension, their breathing is shallow and erratic. This tends to congest the heart energy center and also reduces air vitality and oxygen intake. You can observe the breathing of your family members, co-workers or friends to determine if they are stressed or have emotional concerns.

The chest breathing pattern induces anxiety and emotional overreaction, plus it lowers the lungs' capacity to absorb air. Practice abdominal breathing consciously to reverse this habit or use the internal organs exercise method from the Internal Stamina Exercise (see page 77) to develop a habit of natural abdominal breathing.

SHOULDER BREATHING

The respiratory system and body's own intelligence use shoulder breathing automatically in addition to abdominal breathing to draw in more air when the system needs a tremendous amount of oxygen. After a strenuous physical workout like sprinting or lifting heavy weights, your body demands more oxygen and vitality. Therefore, you tend to experience rapid respiration and deep breathing by expanding your upper trunk and lifting your shoulders.

The problem is that if you do not inflate your abdominal area while doing shoulder and chest breathing, you are compressing the diaphragm instead of maximizing your lung capacity, which pushes the lungs upward, causing less air supply.

Now let's discuss different breathing methods for vitality enhancement and energy management. Before the discussion, see Figure 9 below for the sitting position you will be using for techniques throughout this book.

POSITION FOR BREATHING PRACTICES AND MEDITATION

Figure 9

Seated on a chair with back straight

BREATHE YOUR WAY TO SUCCESS

There are four recommended breathing techniques for vitality and internal stamina development in this chapter. Let's study each one and their benefits. You can do them daily before and after work.

10-5 ABDOMINAL BREATHING TECHNIQUE
Slow abdominal breathing with breath retention is commonly used in yoga and martial arts. This method will increase your vitality rapidly and calm you down, but it is not recommended for pregnant women and people with hypertension or heart ailments.

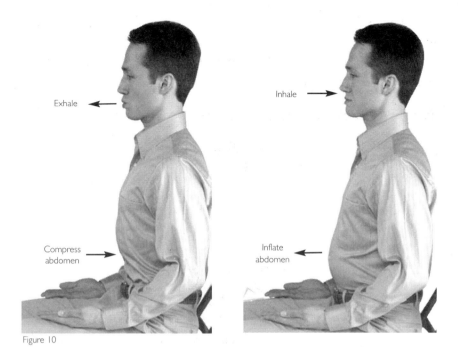

Exhale

Inhale

Compress
abdomen

Inflate
abdomen

Figure 10

Procedure
1. Sit with your spine vertical and your feet flat on the floor.
2. Inhale slowly and deeply into the abdomen while mentally counting to 10.
3. Hold your breath for a count of 5.
4. Exhale slowly, deflating the abdomen completely while mentally counting to 10.
5. Hold your breath for a count of 5.
6. Repeat the whole breathing pattern for a maximum of 5 minutes.
7. Do this procedure 3 times weekly or daily as required.

These abdominal breathing methods have been observed to offer the following benefits:

- De-stress, relax and energetically detoxify yourself
- Revitalize and rejuvenate yourself
- Calm your mind and emotions

COMBINATION BREATHING TECHNIQUE

Apply the following technique to:

- Recover your energy fast during strenuous exercises
- Boost your vitality fast, especially when you are weak or almost fainting
- Revitalize your sexual energy
- Activate your spiritual energy

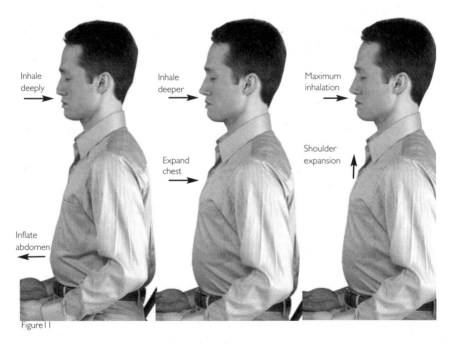

Figure 11

The procedure combines full abdominal, chest and shoulder breathing for maximum air capacity and more time for oxygen and air vitality absorption. This protocol also has spiritual significance for advanced meditators awakening their spiritual powers.

PROCEDURE

1. Sit in a comfortable position with your spine vertical and your feet flat on the floor. You may close your eyes.
2. Place your hands in your lap with your palms facing upward.
3. Inhale slowly and continuously while inflating your abdomen.
4. Continue inhaling slowly, inflating your chest.
5. Continue inhaling slowly until maximum respiration while expanding and lifting your shoulders upwards.
6. Hold your breath steadily for 5 seconds.
7. Exhale all your air slowly while deflating your abdomen and chest, and bring your shoulders back down to their normal position.
8. Hold your breath steadily for 5 seconds.
9. Repeat this breathing process (steps 3-8) only 10 times a maximum of twice a day. Do this 3 times weekly or when high energy is required.

PRECAUTION

This simple breathing technique creates tremendous internal power and a surge of vitality not recommended for pregnant women or people with chest pain, heart ailments, high blood pressure, migraine or headache, glaucoma, cancer or AIDS. If you are not sure, consult your physician before you start this procedure.

SYNCHRONIZED BREATHING METHOD™

The Synchronized Breathing Method is a multipurpose breathing technique to:

- Rapidly release stress
- Calm the emotions and mind fast
- Purify and revitalize the auras and power centers
- Activate and align the energy centers regulating emotional, mental and spiritual energies and faculties

This method was designed after many experiments with the training I received from my early spiritual mentors. Also, while teaching and traveling in India, I encountered several advanced yogis who practice *pranayama yoga*, which literally means "yogic breathing science" in Sanskrit.

Several yogic and healing books also mention two breathing methods: *Kapalabhati pranayama*, which involves rapid inhalation and exhalation with simultaneous up-and-down head movement and *Bastrika pranayama*, which involves rapid compression and expansion of the abdomen during exhalation and inhalation.

Based on my experiments, when I integrated these two breathing styles into one technique, it brought fantastic results: greater detoxifying and revitalizing of the human energy system and rapid calming of the mind and emotions.

I have also added power center breathing to activate and align:

- The heart power center for emotional intelligence
- The mid-brow power center for mental stamina and faculties
- The top-of-head power center for spiritual intelligence and higher inner powers

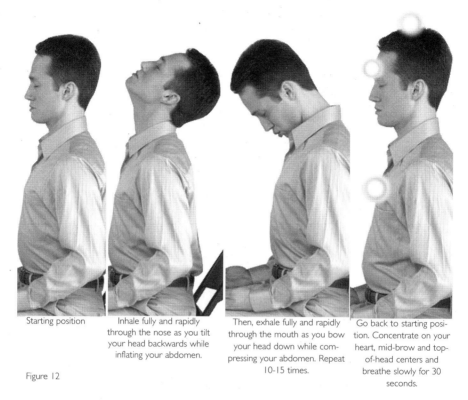

| Starting position | Inhale fully and rapidly through the nose as you tilt your head backwards while inflating your abdomen. | Then, exhale fully and rapidly through the mouth as you bow your head down while compressing your abdomen. Repeat 10-15 times. | Go back to starting position. Concentrate on your heart, mid-brow and top-of-head centers and breathe slowly for 30 seconds. |

Figure 12

PROCEDURE

1. Sit in a comfortable position with your back straight and vertical and your feet flat on the floor. Close your eyes before you start.
2. Inhale fully and rapidly through your nose as you tilt your head backwards while simultaneously inflating your abdomen.
3. Immediately exhale fully and rapidly through your mouth as you bow your head down while compressing your abdomen.
4. Repeat steps 2 and 3 10-15 times.
5. Just relax with your head vertical and breathe slowly. Concentrate on the top-of-head, mid-brow and heart power centers simultaneously while breathing slowly. Do this step for 30 seconds.
6. Repeat steps 2 through 5 three times. You can do this three times weekly or daily as required. Synchronized breathing

followed by nostril breathing (see following page) or combination breathing brings best results.

PRECAUTION

This technique is not recommended for pregnant women or those with neck injuries, high blood pressure, migraine or severe heart conditions. If in doubt, consult your physician before you perform the technique.

HARNESSING THE POWER OF THE SYNCHRONIZED BREATHING METHOD

This method activates the three power centers that stimulate the faculties of love, compassion, creativity, mental stamina, intuition, inspiration, wisdom and global consciousness.

Integrating the rapid breathing and activation of the three energy centers surpasses many methods to detoxify the human energy system, quiet the mind, calm the emotions and bring an overall sense of alignment. This technique has been used successfully by many executives, leaders and teams for stress management, centering and better decision-making.

This method has several practical applications:

1. Businesspeople can clear their emotions and mind before decision-making, negotiating or problem-solving. Mistakes usually occur when you are negatively affected by stress, anxiety, anger, fears and other negative emotions and thoughts.
2. Salespeople and healthcare professionals can create positive energy and powerful presence around their clients. The quality of one's energy — spiritual, mental, emotional and vitality — affects the quality of service offered to clients through energetic osmosis via one's interaction with the client. Our modern times have pushed almost everyone into stressful duties, time constraints, relationship pressures and sometimes even

economic instability. Salespeople and business executives lose many clients because of their negative energy and abrasive presence. Even healthcare workers are stressed and sometimes not emotionally and mentally stable. If the health practitioner is angry, stressed, fearful or has negative energy, it can be transferred to clients or patients.

3. Parents can use this technique to flush out stress and align themselves before going home. You can also release your anger or stress through this fast method before you go to work if your day has started out badly at home.

The Synchronized Breathing Method is recommended for a few minutes before meeting with your clients. Medical practitioners also might want to do this technique a few times daily. Clients and patients deserve to receive a better quality of energy from health professionals to recover faster and get healthier.

Just about everyone can use the Synchronized Breathing Method as a practical tool to maximize performance in work, relationships and spiritual practices. It will also improve your overall health.

Nostril Breathing Technique

Importance of Nostril Breathing

According to ancient teachings in yoga, which I have experimented with extensively and have proven to be effective, if you breathe repeatedly through only one of your nostrils, there are certain outcomes such as:

Right-nostril breathing:
- Increases dynamic activity
- Increases sexual vitality
- Improves digestive functions
- Gives a very optimistic attitude

Slow and very passive people should apply right-nostril breathing daily for about 5 minutes. Sexually over-active or very aggressive people should minimize using this technique. They are already predisposed to a blocked left nostril, and they predominantly breathe with the right nostril daily.

Left-nostril breathing:
- Relaxes and calms you down
- Improves receptiveness and patience
- Gradually helps neutralize aggressiveness and superiority complex
- Provides a more passive and gentle nature

Very gentle and passive people normally are predisposed to left-nostril breathing and generally their right nostril is clogged. Very aggressive and willful people need this breathing technique to calm them down.

You can observe that most healthy people have a natural alternation of breathing, either predominantly through the left or right nostril following what some call the circadian rhythm, which normally alters left and right nostril opening about every 90 minutes throughout the day. The erectile tissues lining the internal nasal passage have this natural intelligence allowing alternate swelling and shrinking to close and open each nostril. If the breathing of the two nostrils balances, you feel a greater inner well-being. Here is the technique to balance the breathing of the two nostrils and balance and flow your more passive and dynamic aspects naturally:

NOSTRIL-CONTROLLED BREATHING TECHNIQUE
This is to improve and balance internal strength (*yang*) and gentle energy (*yin*). Practice for 10 minutes, 3 times weekly.

Preparation

- Sit in a comfortable position with your spine straight and vertical and your feet flat on the floor. Close your eyes for better concentration.
- Do 3 sets of the Synchronized Breathing Method.

Procedure

1. **Right nostril-controlled breathing:**
   Use your right middle finger and thumb to alternately close each nostril.

   a. Close your left nostril with your middle finger and breathe slowly and fully through your right nostril. Hold your breath for 5 seconds.

   b. Simultaneously release your middle finger from the left nostril while closing your right nostril with the thumb. Exhale slowly and completely only through the left nostril. Hold your breath for 5 seconds.

   c. Repeat steps a and b for 3-5 minutes only.
   The goal is to inhale through the right nostril only and exhale through the left nostril only.

2. **Left nostril-controlled breathing:**
   Use your right middle finger and thumb to alternately block each nostril.

   a. Close your right nostril with your thumb and breathe slowly and fully through your left nostril. Hold your breath for 5 seconds.

   b. Simultaneously release your thumb from the right nostril while closing your left nostril with your middle finger. Exhale slowly and completely only through the right nostril. Hold your breath for 5 seconds.

   c. Repeat steps a and b for 3-5 minutes only.

PRECAUTION:

These techniques are not recommended for pregnant women or people with high blood pressure, glaucoma, heart ailments and cancer. The techniques may produce side effects. If in doubt, consult your physician.

You may choose to do only one type of nostril-controlled breathing to improve or correct any tendencies of extreme passivity or aggression. If you want to balance your more passive and willful natures, you can spend equal time on both types of breathing or a little bit more on one type depending on what you want to decrease or increase. (Refer back to the discussion on pages 99-100 regarding what qualities each side of nostril-controlled breathing gives.) When the breathing from both nostrils is balanced, your gentler and more dynamic qualities flow more smoothly and naturally for an integrated approach to decision-making, problem-solving, negotiating and relationships.

The techniques to enhance vitality are a simple science. We have assembled the techniques into menus or methods applied to various requirements. You can choose different techniques for specific applications. But there are at least four important techniques recommended weekly to maximize your performance and balance the Triangle of Success and Fulfillment – will-power, love and creative intelligence – as follows:

a. Internal Stamina Exercise (daily or 3 times weekly)
b. Synchronized Breathing Method (daily or 3 times weekly)
c. 10-5 abdominal breathing or combination breathing (daily or 3 times weekly, preferably after Internal Stamina Exercise)
d. Nostril-controlled breathing (3 times weekly, especially after Synchronized Breathing)

Note: These methods can be done independently, but best results can be achieved when they are integrated according to the weekly schedules in chapter 9.

For more advanced techniques to develop will-power, study and apply the methods in chapter 7, pages 188-192

When you master this chapter's techniques, you substantially master your vitality and the ability to develop more will-power. Vitality mastery and management are not just about adding energy. Vitality enhancement is more than just building physical muscles or strength. Sometimes we need to subtract toxic energy first, like stress and negative feelings and thoughts, then add positive energy and vitality. We need to include a regimen to restore vitality and stamina fast by releasing stress, tension and fatigue in just a few minutes. Isn't that what you've been looking for: fast, simple and effective? You've got it!

The vitality component of success – the secret behind the will-power aspect of the Success and Fulfillment Triangle – is what most people need, whether young or old, healthy or sick, dynamic or depressed. Success is hard to achieve and maintain without good health, vitality and will-power. This chapter is designed to meet the needs of healthy individuals to become even healthier and more successful. It's also designed for less healthy people so they can recover faster and get back on the road to success. The methods have been created to be simple, easy-to-apply and ready-to-use without needing special gadgets, clothing or places to practice. I encourage you to try practicing them weekly as part of your path to a happier, healthier life.

CHAPTER 5

HOW LOVE FUELS SUCCESS
AND FULFILLMENT

◆

The next key to your success and fulfillment in our universal model after will-power is a more developed love nature by developing your emotional faculties. Love serves as a main catalyzing ingredient to transform success into fulfillment for the following reasons:

- ◆ Love, joy, inner peace and contentment create the feeling of self-fulfillment that is beyond the satisfaction of mere success.
- ◆ Positive emotional virtues of benevolence and altruism guiding material and financial success will bring sustained abundance and social influence. These virtues transform a rich person to become a legend by creating a philanthropic focus.
- ◆ Love gives the sense of conscience for win-win decision-making, problem-solving and negotiating. The win-win approach entitles you to better and long-lasting results in life.
- ◆ The love virtue expressed through kindness, compassion and inclusiveness brings you more harmonious relationships, personal magnetism and great circles of positive influence in life.

Inspirational Leadership Through Emotional Intelligence

Emotional intelligence is expressed through love and devotion to others, great ideals and goals, accompanied by compassion and understanding. It is also a manifestation of the power of the heart that discriminates right from wrong, which we normally call conscience. The higher aspects of emotional intelligence and faculties lead successful people to great achievements.

Magnetism is another emotional faculty, which results in the quality and ability to be liked by people and, if you are a leader, to be cherished by your followers or team. A great influential leader is not made powerful just by their expertise or power derived through position or office.

Let's look at a well-known figure as an example. We can learn through her style of using not only talent but also the power of emotional intelligence to achieve success and fulfillment. Often, this type of person is not even aware of these faculties.

Mother Teresa is an example of using the power of emotional intelligence as a natural tool to be liked by many and have a big social impact. Many in the media and the international public loved Mother Teresa, who devoted her life to helping the poor in India and other countries through many projects. Her compassionate nature even made her a candidate for canonization as a saint by the Catholic church. Her powers of servant leadership, benevolence and compassion have left a legacy.

Power of Love, Compassion and Conscience

This higher emotional power is a transformation of the love of things, goals and personalities into a higher intention and motive to use love for greater service and better relationships. It involves not only the quality of the heart, but also the unconditional love expressed by the top-of-head power center. If a person's desires and prayers are limited to personality or family needs, the development of emotional energy takes place in the heart and solar plexus energy centers. The solar plexus power center is where personality and self-interests are stimulated, involving physical appetites, but also including the virtue of courage. Courage is an emotional force supported by strong ideals.

Once a person starts evolving and the heart center is more active, intentions and prayers become wishes or invocations for groups, the community good, organizations, cities, countries and humanity as a whole.

When the top-of-head power center is developed, it culminates in the selfless sacrifice and service for the good of humanity and the Earth. Thus, a person who has well-developed top-of-head and heart centers has integrated the faculties of global consciousness, wisdom, intuition, inspiration and unconditional love.

> *I know myself now,*
> *and I feel within me*
> *a peace above all earthly dignities,*
> *a still and quiet conscience.*
> William Shakespeare, English playwright[3]

This can be seen energetically as the top-of-head power center opening like a crown. The symbols of spiritual power and enlightenment are the crown of the Christ and the Buddha, the miter of the Pope and the many-feathered headdress of Native American shamans.

The powers of love, compassion and aspiration are the higher counterparts of passion. Many people begin with passion, but as they evolve into more advanced human beings, they guide their lives with aspiration, compassion and all-inclusiveness. At this high-level expression of heart and top-of-head center development, great human beings always leave humanity and the world a legacy of monumental projects and service. Compassion and aspiration leading to inspiration are the qualities of Saints and Sages that lubricate their world service.

So what are the common emotional qualities of the greatest world leaders? Let's look at some of those shared by the Christ, the Buddha and founders of religions, as well as Mahatma Gandhi, Mother Teresa and some modern science and business leaders.

Universal love:
Love exceeding love for self, family, friends, country and culture

Compassion for all life:
Not only for humanity but for all species of nature

Inner peace, leading to serenity:
Undisturbed continuous peace

Continuous joy, leading to bliss:
A deep experience attributed to the fulfillment of one's higher destiny and life's purpose

Altruism:
A natural gift to give and share selflessly

Benevolence:
A selfless act of love and kindness

Conscience:
The power to feel what is right and wrong through your heart

How do we know emotional intelligence really exists? Almost everyone can feel a pleasant, warm opening feeling in the heart when doing good things for others. But when a person has emotional intelligence and happens to harm someone, either through negative thoughts, feelings or actions, the result can be a shrinking, heavy, unpleasant feeling in the heart or chest area. Thus the power of conscience can be used as a faculty to feel what is right and wrong.

When the heart center is very developed and open, the person is always loving and very sensitive to the needs of others, resulting in a natural expression of compassion. When the compassionate act or expression is extended to a greater influence and global cause, the top-of-head center starts to develop further, resulting in universal love and global service. This inner transformation converts success into greater fulfillment accompanied by global contribution.

The powers of the heart are extremely important to all roles in your life – in your home and family, your work and career, your spiritual life and duty, your environmental and community contributions and your health.

The emotional intelligence of the heart is best expressed as follows:

The heart has a reason that reason knows nothing of.
Blaise Pascal, French mathematician and philosopher

Power of Emotional Magnetism and Presence

Have you ever heard the expression, "You are very magnetic"? We've all heard of people with magnetic sex appeal. This appeal is created by a charismatic aura. Emotional magnetic presence can be classified into the following types:

- ◆ Sex appeal
- ◆ Charismatic emotional magnetism or presence
- ◆ Combination of both sexual and charismatic magnetism, which results in the ability to draw people not just with verbal communication skills, good looks or good public relations. In fact, some charismatic people don't have to speak at all to inspire others. People tend to stay with them because they feel good in their presence.

The real ability to be effective in business transactions depends on how people feel about you. In most cases, the charisma of the salesperson influences our choices as much as the quality of the goods or services. The same goes for recruiting and hiring new employees, especially if you are hiring an assistant or important workers in your organization. It's how you feel about the new hire that matters in the end. Therefore, maintaining a pleasant-feeling, radiating, positive energy and emotional charisma in daily life is very important for relationships, business and careers.

Most business and public relations training has been based on pleasing the customer and serving the client. The ability to project a good feeling and sincerity in our service is determined by the real inner feelings of the heart center and the vibration of the emotional aura. A developed heart center naturally exudes pleasant feelings and allows one to perform great service building server-customer-client relationships naturally.

On the other hand, people who are not as developed have smaller heart centers, so it is hard for them to forgive and forget the pains of life and negative experiences. They do not have as much heart or loving substance to draw upon. People with small heart centers also get stressed more easily because perception is more pessimistic when the solar plexus center is over-activated and the heart center is not flowing.

Kristina Gunther, our brilliant but socially-challenged technology research director from chapter 2, is a good example of what happens to many professionals with smaller heart centers. Too much mental intelligence without heart contributes to Kristina's stress, loneliness, aloofness and suffering in life. Typically with professionals like Kristina, relationships are either absent or strained because a smart person without the inclusiveness of the heart tends to attract conflict rather than cooperation or doesn't invest time in building social relationships.

Many businesspeople are successful for a time because they are fueled by the passion, commitment and determination brought by the drive of the solar plexus power center. But their strong solar plexus power center can also make them stressful to be around, impatient and abrasive.

You cannot give what you do not have inside.
Love, compassion and forgiveness can only be given
when the heart is filled with these positive qualities.

People who are considered "big-hearted" are more patient and understanding, so they have greater stress tolerance, better performance and more fulfilling relationships. Estella Walsh, our popular educator case study from chapter 2, is the opposite of Kristina Gunther. Her big heart makes people trust her and want to be around her instinctively.

To perform well in both professional and personal life over the long term, more emotional magnetism and intelligence combined with a highly developed mind and constant will-power and vitality are needed.

KNOW YOURSELF: Rate your current level of emotional intelligence qualities. Rate 0 to 4.	DEVELOP YOURSELF: Where would you like to be in 6 months? Rate 0 to 4.
Sense of inner peace and contentment ____	Sense of inner peace and contentment ____
Emotional instincts ____	Emotional instincts ____
Win-win outcomes sought in decision-making ____	Win-win outcomes sought in decision-making ____
Kindness, compassion and inclusiveness ____	Kindness, compassion and inclusiveness ____
Many friends and good relationships ____	Many friends and good relationships ____
Emotional magnetism ____	Emotional magnetism ____

How to Open Your Heart

The following techniques to culture greater love and a more open heart offer the benefits of:

- Minimal or no stress in your daily performance
- Enhanced personal and group relationships
- Better rapport with people
- Magnetic appeal that greatly enhances your external and internal effectiveness and inner beauty
- A wholesome presence, triggered by a pleasant emotional aura
- Power of the heart as your discriminating conscience for truth
- A life full of love, harmony and peace
- Power of compassion to guide your material success

Some people's temperaments are not naturally gifted with a loving nature like Mother Teresa. However, you can develop greater love and open your heart through the following techniques, even if you're more mental:

1. Inner emotional purification breathing method to expel and remove negative emotional tendencies, feelings and vibrations
2. Activating the heart power center to stimulate the love nature
3. Substituting and adding positive emotional attitudes and virtues through affirmations and visualizations

Inner Emotional Purification and Revitalization Method (5 minutes)
PROCEDURE

1.   Imagine yourself in front of an ocean and expel all negative feelings and emotions by breathing them out. Just have the intention that the ocean is absorbing them. It is easier to release negativity when you exhale out to a target like the ocean.

2.   Do deep and slow breathing for about 5 minutes, relax and let go. Breathe out the negative feelings and emotions listed below. Repeated inner breathing to externalize these negative tendencies will disempower their influence on your consciousness:

   a. Stress and emotional tension to improve your performance

   b. Fear, worries and phobias that reduce your vitality and weaken your power. Removing them always enhances your virtues and growth.

   c. Irritability, anger or hatred. These deactivate and inhibit your emotional and mental faculties and negatively influence your relationships. These negative attitudes drain you and create enemies.

   d. Jealousy, envy or lack of confidence. These corrupt relationships and slow down your performance. Releasing them allows you to enjoy inner peace and self-esteem and builds trust in relationships.

   e. Compulsive behaviors and obsessions. These destroy your life and health, especially if they result in vices. Releasing them will enable you to enjoy your good health and future and will give you the ability to regulate your life.

   f. Selfishness and greed. Releasing them gives you the power to continuously materialize and enjoy abundance without mishaps connected to wealth.

SCHEDULE

I suggest doing all of the following techniques at least three times a week and whenever you need a more positive attitude and emotional power.

Emotional Revitalization (5 minutes, 3 times a week)

Removing or subtracting the negative emotional attitudes and emotional behaviors by externalizing negative energies that trigger them is not enough. To avoid relapse from the negative tendencies, you need to substitute positive emotional energies and programs into your emotional aura and consciousness.

PROCEDURE

1. Concentrate on the heart and top-of-head power centers simultaneously while breathing slowly and deeply (2 minutes).
2. Affirmation (7 times):
   Continue the inner breathing and do the following affirmation 7 times:

   I am a peaceful, loving and harmonious person.
   I am a being of love. Love, I am.

3. Visualize the positive emotional attitudes or virtues of loving relationships, kindness, compassion, generosity, loving understanding, harmony and peace as part of your daily life for 2 minutes.

Rapid Inner Purification and Revitalization Method (7 minutes)

If you need to remove negative emotions or stress quickly, this is a more complete technique that yields fast, wonderful results to quiet your mind, calm your emotions and stimulate a positive emotional attitude. This method can be used instead of the first two techniques.

You are encouraged to experience it immediately before going on to the next topic.

PROCEDURE: 3 times a week or as needed

1. Synchronized Breathing Method (3 sets) (see pages 96-99).
2. Silently affirm (7 times):

I am a peaceful, loving and harmonious person.
I am a being of love. Love, I am.

3. Visualize the positive emotional attitudes or virtues of loving relationships, kindness, compassion, generosity, loving understanding, harmony and peace as part of your daily life for 3 minutes.

As you practice the techniques and recommendations from this chapter, I hope they will bring you emotional well-being and the power of love that improves and sustains your ability to be loved, allowing your social influence, leadership, success and fulfillment to grow even further.

The methods were created with simplicity and a straightforward approach to suit very busy individuals who have only 5-10 minutes a day to practice. The three techniques in this chapter will reduce stress and difficulties by detoxifying the emotional and mental pollutants that you absorb from other people and the environment. Doing the techniques is like taking an emotional bath to refresh your feelings. Life is good. You should enjoy it more. Continue the practice and keep nurturing the power of your heart to bring more success and fulfillment to your life.

CHAPTER 6

CREATIVE INTELLIGENCE:
BECOME A MENTAL POWERHOUSE

The third component of the Success and Fulfillment Triangle is creative intelligence, expressed as the power of the mind. The power of the mind is needed to envision, build, create and materialize goals, vision, strategies and solutions and to analyze options.

Will-power without mental faculties tends to impose crystallized, inflexible ideas and dogmas. Love without mental power is not practical, discriminating or intelligently applied.

Without the building nature of creative intelligence, love has nothing to preserve and will-power has nothing to destroy for new creation. The cycle is incomplete. Thus the Success and Fulfillment Triangle requires the third element of creative intelligence to complete and balance the will-power and love.

Many of today's businesspeople are very smart, innovative and creative, constantly improving existing processes or rapidly actualizing new concrete ways to meet needs. But in my experience, even the smartest are currently still only using a small percentage of the advanced human mental faculties available today. What's needed is integrated concrete and abstract thinking, with more conscience of the heart to discern options and intuitive faculties to be a real visionary. This integration will make you a mental powerhouse.

The current problem-solving and decision-making nature of business lends itself to employing certain mental faculties, but are most people's solutions and decisions today really visionary? Is it possible for businesspeople, leaders, scientists, inventors, politicians, artists, physicians and policymakers to see even further ahead with more pioneering ideas and solutions? What do you think? How original is your thinking? Would you gain a valuable edge in your professional and personal life if you had techniques to become more of a mental powerhouse?

In order to develop creative intelligence further and use the mind properly, we need to explore how the mind works and the various functions, faculties and powers of the mind like critical thinking, innovation, creativity, imagination, focus and awareness and the ability to materialize goals.

Two Aspects of the Mind:
CONCRETE AND ABSTRACT

Your concrete mind deals with sequential, logical, normal reasoning and concrete thinking faculties. Your abstract mind is responsible for the more subjective, creative, philosophical and principle-based thinking faculties and processes.

The mind is the human mechanism or energy software to think. Your mind is an energy field that, like radio systems, has different frequency bands, from a lower vibrational signal to a very high signal. This energy field can be called a "mental aura" that produces thoughts and receives thoughts from others.

When people have developed and used much of their concrete thinking, such as engineers and physicists, the next step is to develop and stimulate the abstract mind. The abstract mental level is where you can connect to higher creative ideas, noble principles and universal philosophies resulting in a more abstract understanding and creative expression of life.

MIND VERSUS THE BRAIN

The mind is composed of a person's mental energy field or aura operating with a combination of functions like a receiver, transmitter, condenser and computer. The mind can receive, store, assimilate and process, then transmit information or data. The brain is the limited hardware for the mind (software) to use for receiving, processing and transmitting signals, which are the thoughts. Cellular phones, TV and radio equipment exemplify the functions of the mind. The people who made these inventions possible are really admirable.

The mental faculties are usually physicalized through the functions of the current left and right brain model, which limits the complete analysis of how the mind works. This theory assigns the left brain to the concrete thinking mechanism and the right brain to the subjective, abstract and creative mechanism. This is familiar to many people. But the proponents of this idea equate the mind with the brain instead of classifying the mind as the software and receiver, processor, storer and transmitter of data and the brain as the hardware or physical equipment.

We will not elaborate much on the physiology and anatomy of the brain here. That is the specialization of medical science and much attention, research and products have already been developed for its benefit. Instead, we will emphasize the mental faculties, their development and applications for present needs and future requirements applied to success and fulfillment.

To study and understand the faculty of your mind more deeply, let's see how your thoughts and manifestations of reality are related, or how your mind is utilized to physicalize or affect the outcomes of events such as a fulfilled life.

How Your Mind, Brain and Thoughts Are Related

How do your thoughts and thinking habits affect your physical body and its vitality and chemistry? Let's do several experiments.

EXPERIMENT:

The Effects of Your Mind and Thoughts on Your Physical Body and Its Chemistry

> Close your eyes and visualize that you are in your kitchen. Go to the refrigerator and take out an orange. Slice it into two halves. Open your mouth and squeeze the juice into your mouth many times. Let the juice stay in your mouth. How does it taste? What is the effect on your salivary glands? Is there an effect of visualization or imagination? How did this thought affect your body and its chemistry?

Imagine a fearful situation or negative event in your life, whether real or not: How does it affect your body and stimulate certain hormonal reactions? In my experience with clients, there is a direct effect.

This also explains why the power of the mind, expressed through techniques like affirmations and visualization, helps heal the body and emotions and increase vitality. On the other hand, a person with negative thinking habits can also devitalize their emotional and physical health through negative thinking and undermine their ability to achieve goals, success and fulfillment.

What do you think? What adjustments do you need to make in your thought patterns to create a healthier, more successful and fulfilled life?

Let's try another experiment.

EXPERIMENT:
How Your Mind, Emotions and Vitality Are Related

> Close your eyes again and think of an enemy or critic. If you do not have one, think of a person who hurt you deeply and focus on the event or how negative the person is. Do this for 2 minutes.
>
> What's the effect on your emotions and vitality? Did you become devitalized, depressed or agitated? What is the effect on your feelings and heart center? Did your stomach or solar plexus center react? What's the effect on your breathing? Did it become shallow and erratic? What's the effect on your heartbeat?

With these experiments and results, we can conclude that repeated or prolonged negative thoughts drain your vitality and negatively affect your emotions and health. Therefore, if the mind can heal, the mind can also harm.

Now the benefit of having a more refined and advanced mind should be clearer. Culturing the mind goes beyond book learning, earning degrees and being intellectual. Advanced mental development externalizes as positive, powerful, cultured words and behavior, which create good relationships and a very successful life.

On the other hand, since contemplating negative experiences, events or people brings us down, it is wise to avoid it. If we think negatively, we are not refining our mental energy, but are contaminating it. Gossip and criticizing others have the same effect, and we attract to ourselves the very things we are criticizing due to energetic osmosis.

You cannot throw mud at others
without dirtying your own hands first.

THE MAGICAL POWERS OF THE MIND

Let's do another experiment.

EXPERIMENT:
How the Power of Your Mind Can Materialize Your Goals Fast

Do this standing up with your feet apart at shoulder width. Stay in this position until the experiment is done. People with back, hip or knee problems should not do this experiment. Try to touch the floor or ground as low as you can without bending your knees. Do not over-exert! Remember how low you have extended your fingers towards the floor and how easy or difficult it was. Now, go back to the standing position with closed eyes and visualize that you have touched the floor or ground lower and easier than before. Repeat the visualizations 7 times. Again, try to touch the floor as low as you can. Evaluate the level and feel the difference of the effort and ease compared to the first try. Do another set of visualization 7 times and imagine that you are even more flexible and extending your fingers even lower towards the floor. Try to physically touch the floor and compare it with your first attempts.

Is there an improvement? In just a few seconds of visualizing the goal, what is the effect of your mind in achieving the goal? Did it improve your performance? Did you achieve better results with your objective?

I used to train and coach martial arts teams for competition ranging from beginner levels for men, women and children to black belt all weight divisions. We usually ended our training with a meditation and concentration to visualize the results we wanted. By teaching this mental programming to my team members and repeating these techniques many times a few weeks before competitions, we often won the team championships. There is truth in the saying:

What we think repeatedly of ourselves, we become.

The goals we repeatedly think about and focus on tend to materialize faster and easier. Therefore, spend time mentally visualizing or concentrating on positive end results only.

If you think of negative outcomes, especially accompanied by or resulting in fears and worries, determine if they are real or if your mind is reminding you of potential difficulties. This is a normal occurrence, but do not dwell on problems too long. Instead, create solutions and have contingency plans.

Avoid creating goals and making decisions when you are not in a good emotional mood or if you are very angry, stressed or fearful. Why? Because the perception of what is urgent and right in this state is not necessarily correct.

When people create goals and intentions colored by negative emotions, the goals and outcomes may seem valid at the time, but in the long run, they can boomerang as suffering and destructive effects. In creating goals and mental intentions, always countercheck yourself with role-reversals and apply the Golden Rule.

THE GOLDEN RULE
Do unto others what you want others to do unto you.
Do not do unto others what you do not want others to do unto you.

Confucius, Chinese philosopher

The Koran also states the following:

Noblest religion this — that thou shouldst like for others
what thou likest for thyself; and what thou findest painful for thyself,
hold that as painful for all others too.
As ye would that men should do unto you, do ye also to them likewise.

The Koran, Book of Islam

When you observe the businesspeople who have been accused of attempts to defraud stockholders and other types of less positive activity, it is easy to see that as one becomes mentally sharper and smarter, many things can be manipulated and justified to seem correct or right. The problem is that this can result in short-term success followed by a lifetime of regret or suffering. It would be wise to remember the lessons of Oscar Wayne from chapter 2, the successful real estate business leader with plenty of vices, stress and a heart attack at 48 before he transformed into a very fulfilled person. Therefore, be careful when creating powerful thoughts, intentions and goals.

How to Maximize the Use of Your Mind

To become a mental powerhouse and maximize your faculties of creative intelligence, you need to know four current maximum uses of your mind. They are:

- ◆ Common sense
- ◆ High grade of common sense
- ◆ The concrete mind
- ◆ The abstract mind

Many professionals currently use common sense and the concrete mind; the next step is to tap into a high grade of common sense and bring more vision and understanding through abstract thinking.

Common Sense Is For Mediocre Thinking

In ordinary people, common sense is a body of reasoning using knowledge or feedback through the five senses. More intelligent people use the concrete mind to process data, and less intelligent people use the emotional instincts. Therefore, the reliability of the conclusion depends on the intelligence of the mind and emotions to interpret the perceived data. Because common sense generally depends on old conclusions, history or existing data, there is a danger of tapping into mixed truth and false information. Perceptions based on false data exist, which seem to appear true and are justified as correct because of the "veils" of negative old programming or beliefs. Also, people's emotions and minds are immersed in or connected to many oceans of existing thoughts, ideas and emotional programs. This is why common sense is very useful for someone with good discrimination, but it is not reliable for someone who is very emotionally impulsive and non-discriminating.

To give a bigger picture, let's explore the elements of common sense and how it is developed.

ELEMENTS OF MASS COMMON SENSE

- Ideas and knowledge from previous cultures, civilizations and races
- Knowledge from science
- Teachings from education and religion
- Beliefs and superstitions of any kind from all sources
- Illusions of thinkers and groups
- Media information, which can be true, false or partially correct
- Experience from upbringing and daily life

Every day, this body of common sense is building up through the aggregate of humanity's thoughts and emotions, especially now that we have global connectedness through media and Internet use. The problem arises when these mental and emotional programs and powerful streams of information called mass common sense feed people's minds with wrong input. This leads to wrong conclusions and wrong decisions that make people suffer and fail. Therefore, guidelines are needed for the proper use of common sense.

GUIDELINES FOR THE PROPER USE OF COMMON SENSE

- *Be open-minded, but not fanatical* in believing all the things you read, hear or see. Always ask questions regarding the what, why and how of anything. It is helpful to see the bigger picture rather than believing everything.
- *Be careful with gossip and news,* either from the media or personal conversation. Anything not useful to your life, which brings separativeness or failure should be cast aside or dismissed. Validate information and investigate the truth if you are concerned with the given information or news. Extract what is true and useful and ignore wrong data.
- *Use scientific data or opinions from experts* as much as possible.
- *Do not rush to conclusions* if in doubt. Assess common sense with hunches or physical and emotional instincts.
- *Use reliable historical data* to validate common sense.
- *Seek advice from a consultant or expert* on the subject matter to avoid unnecessary mistakes. Get a second or third opinion if in doubt.
- *Only read good books* or materials from a variety of reliable sources to avoid admitting more false data into your mental files or emotional memory and to be well-rounded in different subjects.
- *Seek out brilliant and successful people* and look for groups of them to associate with. Good common sense is contagious through group interaction.
- *Approach things with a more universal sense* when confronted with conflicting information since your perception is based on your emotional and mental analysis, which has preferences or biases.
- *Be detached from your usual likes and dislikes* if you are deciding for a group. Remove biases by prioritizing what is best for your group or team.
- *Know your weaknesses and strengths.* When making decisions, know where your common sense or reasoning is coming from, and be fair and realistic. Do not allow decision-making and reason to be colored by old sentiments, personal grievances or negative motives. Use role-reversal to test for win-win situations.

- *Values and virtues* are helpful in situations where your reasoning is doubtful. Applying the universal values of life guarantees that you are right even if your common sense dictates differently.
- *Be realistic.* Know the real facts and recognize what is practical and objective. Shift to mental reason when you become too emotional or sentimental. Use the right criteria according to short- and long-term goals, aligned to a higher purpose.

The power of your common sense depends on the state of your emotional and mental development and on the degree to which your spiritual values are developed. Therefore, a lifetime of building character and culturing the emotions and mind is the reliable path to mastery of common sense for many people.

KNOW YOURSELF:
How much do you use common sense in your daily life?

	Yes	No
I study how others did things historically in my profession before me.	___	___
I study books, articles and audios on trends in my profession.	___	___
I studied my profession in school.	___	___
I base many of my conclusions on media coverage.	___	___
I use my own past experience for decision-making.	___	___
My principles are guided by my family and cultural upbringing.	___	___
I tend to have superstitious beliefs.	___	___
I use my religious doctrine and beliefs as my guide.	___	___
I rely solely on expert opinions.	___	___

If you answered "yes" to several of the questions, then you are probably using a lot of common sense for your mental reasoning.

Smarter People Use A High Grade of Common Sense

Higher faculties supersede normal reasoning in advanced people. Developing the abstract mind is the next step for most of humanity in order to transcend the illusion and confusion of mass thought, which can muddy decision-making, problem-solving and negotiating, especially in business. Therefore, many professionals will eventually progress to the next stage of mental development, the abstract mind.

A high grade of common sense is a more powerful mental faculty than common sense. More learned people born with a better apprehension of life from the time they were young are equipped with a high grade of common sense. They are not necessarily degree holders or those educated in schools.

One factor that makes them better thinkers is an extra faculty of inner sensitivity that allows them to experience truth faster than most people. They also have greater exposure to and interaction with intelligent and wise people. These intelligent and wise individuals may be their parents, coaches, mentors or spiritual teachers.

Many great personalities have been exposed to great and successful people and leaders, so through energetic osmosis and "positive contamination" of qualities, they acquire a higher grade of common sense and intelligence.

Children also become more intelligent by observing smart people and parents. In fact, some people with this faculty do not have degrees or a formal academic education. And some drop out of school because they are bored or prefer to learn differently.

A HIGH GRADE OF COMMON SENSE:
The Bill Gates Story

> Bill Gates is a good example of a high grade of common sense. He dropped out of Harvard University to co-found Microsoft in 1975. Currently, he continues to head up that company and has been assessed as the world's richest man. According to David Gelernter who wrote for *Time*, "Gates is the Bing Crosby of American technology, borrowing a tune here and a tune there and turning them all into great boffo hits[4]". Gelernter continues: "The Gates Road to Wealth is still a one-laner, and traffic is limited. But the idea that a successful corporation should enrich not merely its executives and stockholders, but also a fair number of ordinary line employees is potentially revolutionary[5]".
>
> Many accuse Bill Gates of monopoly. Others see him as an idol. Regardless of how he is perceived, he has a high grade of common sense that many very educated people lack.

I have observed in many of my clients, friends and acquaintances that a high grade of common sense can be developed by international travel and especially by living in different cultures. Even with intense training from my early spiritual mentors and deep study of advanced books from the Eastern Wisdom, my knowledge and common sense about religions and cultures would have been more theoretical and idealistic without having lived and worked in Asia, the Middle East, India, North, South and Central America and Europe. With travels to other countries to experience the different cultures of these places, one gains a deeper understanding of why we exist today as such – and harmony through contrast and unity through diversity become wise ideas.

In addition to exposure to various cultures and having a good mentor, the opportunity to mingle or work with brilliant people, especially leaders, is one of the fastest ways to acquire a high grade of common sense. Most highly intelligent leaders have this virtue, but it has to be progressively and continuously developed and refined. For today's leaders and decision-makers, this is one of the most important faculties to develop for now.

KNOW YOURSELF:
How much of your high grade of common sense
do you use in your daily life?

	Yes	No
I actively seek out and surround myself with smart, experienced people.		
I study and adopt the successful strategies of great and successful people.		
I prefer non-linear ways of learning and action.		
I have traveled to many different countries and have more global consciousness.		
I have experienced other cultures first-hand and have realized the beauty of diversity.		
I have a mentor or mentors.		
I have a well-rounded approach to decisions and consider the expertise of others.		
I don't rely on media, publicity and gossip without discernment.		
I usually validate complex information as much as possible.		
I believe in first-hand information from experts, but I solicit a second opinion.		
I am aware of the beauty and value of many different religious teachings and I sense that each of them has different levels of truth.		
I continue to upgrade and evaluate what I know is right.		

If you answered "yes" to serveral of the questions,
then you are probably using a high grade of common sense for your mental
reasoning.

YOUR CONCRETE MIND

Scientists (especially physicists), lawyers, engineers and accountants are experts in concrete thinking power. The detailed and organized search for truth is an active faculty of the throat power center and considered a left-brain process, although more advanced scientists and engineers also start to incorporate the abstract mind and right-brain processes. In ordinary people, the concrete mind is starting to develop. Most of our education systems today still focus on concrete mind development. Our schools tend to emphasize memorization and deductive learning. Even our world history is taught through memorization instead of understanding and abstraction of human lessons in order to recognize which mistakes not to repeat in the future.

Many advanced children are bored in school. Sometimes they are classified as having Attention Deficit Disorder or ADHD. While some children classified as Attention Deficit Disorder or ADHD do have difficulty processing information, others are reacting to the ordinary, slow, linear learning environment. For some of them, their minds may be faster than their age group and they need to occupy some mental gaps by doing something else or by thinking on a different frequency with different intentions.

I have worked with children and adult clients who are labeled Attention Deficit Disorder (ADD), but who have developed minds. I also had classmates who excelled in math, but performed poorly in arts. They were so-called left-brain people. People who are sometimes called geeks and nerds seem to have partially developed very good concrete mental faculties, but lack emotional development. That's why they can be geniuses with concrete mental expertise, but without the ability to relate to others emotionally.

THOUGHTS VERSUS EMOTIONS

How does the concrete mind work and gain its power? The concrete mind creates thoughts and ideas usually deduced from common sense information or through a logical, sequential thinking process. Another important point is that thoughts are not feelings and vice-versa. The substance forming thoughts is more refined than the emotional or feeling substance. Here are some examples and processes:

PROCESS	CREATED	CREATING MECHANISM
Think of a green apple	Visual images of the green apple	Concrete mind
Have a desire to eat it	Emotional appetite called desire	Emotional aura
Experience and feel the event	Emotional feeling about the event	Predominantly emotional aura
Visualize and think of your brain	Visuals and thoughts about the brain	Concrete mind (not the brain)

People from different cultures with different languages create "thoughtforms" or visual images with the same forms and features. For example, a North American says and mentally thinks "apple" and a South American says and mentally thinks "manzana", but the mental energy created by both has the same visual form. This is the basis of mind reading and telepathy.

Thoughts come from the mind,
and feelings emanate from the emotions.

YOUR ABSTRACT MIND AND THE POWER OF "WHY"?

We've discussed the functions and faculties of the concrete mind. What comes next? Abstract mental power. Abstract, subjective, philosophical, principle-based thinking belongs to the abstract mind.

The new modern generations are more equipped with the power of the abstract mind. You can observe how many advanced children learn new things. They ask you questions starting with, "What is this"? and "How is it"? and usually end with, "Why does this exist"? The questions of "what"? and "how"? are an exercise of the concrete mind to accumulate knowledge and express the idea practically. When the point of interest is the why's of life, then the abstract mental faculty is being stimulated.

Another training tool for this higher mental faculty is asking questions that have not been experienced or known by the concrete mind or which have no logical meaning. For instance, in Zen training, the enlightened teacher called a *Roshi* gives his students *koans* or puzzles to be contemplated for a long time before arriving at an appropriate answer. I did not say correct answer because it is not really the concrete accuracy of the mind that has the answer but the abstract faculty to discover the answer.

Here's a familiar Zen *koan*: What is the sound of one hand clapping? Try using the reasoning of the concrete mind: The memory does not recognize any experience, and it cannot comprehend unexperienced non-linear concepts with deductions, so it relinquishes the thinking power to the abstract mind, which will search for the philosophical answer, concept or principle. So the answer is not always a straightforward statement. Try another abstract mind training puzzle and observe how your mind reacts: Which came first, the chicken or the egg? Ponder on this and observe your mental faculties and processes.

Another difference between your concrete mind and your abstract mind is that your concrete mind uses a focusing and concentrating technique while your abstract mind uses the techniques of awareness and understanding faculties. When you say, "I know", you are using the concrete mind, but when you say, "I understand", you are using the abstract mind.

Techniques to train your abstract mind further are given later in this chapter.

HOW YOUR MIND WORKS

To understand how your mind works, we need to study in detail the functions, faculties and powers of the mind from the most concrete to abstract levels.

FUNCTIONS, FACULTIES AND POWERS OF YOUR MIND

- Information storage and memory
- Organizing, decision-making and problem-solving
- Research, investigation and mental analysis
- Concretizing ideas
- Innovation and creativity
- Imagination
- Focus and awareness

HOW YOU MEMORIZE AND STORE INFORMATION IN YOUR MIND

Your concrete mind memorizes and stores information. Your brain does not store data. Your brain is the hardware used to process information when data are first registered. If you recall information, you draw from the data bank, which is the mental aura.

There are energy compartments or memory banks in your concrete mind that serve as repositories of information or data. The grosser the thought, the lower the frequency at which it is stored. The more refined the idea, the higher the frequency at which it will be assimilated. I call these "mental diskettes" or energy compartments.

Your mental aura and its energy substance need purifying and decongesting. This mental system is like the data storage unit in our computers. We need to purge unnecessary or obsolete data or documents to the recycling bin or trash regularly. There are also obsolete data from our younger years and previous training that have to be erased or purged when they have become irrelevant or obsolete. Then the new data and updated valid information should replace or supersede the old obsolete information. In the future, these techniques will be utilized in the new education for new generations. Today, they are taught in our workshops with the hope that they will eventually be used by educators and other professionals globally as a technology to develop super-learning faculties.

People become so confused with conflicting information in their decision-making because early exposure to fairy tales, fables, parables and early limiting conclusions about life are still intact and competing with the more realistic adult interpretation of life. This is the internal tension in people who grapple with conflicting ideas of archetypal models of truth and their own repeated valid experience. They don't know how to behave in expressing the higher truth currently perceived because of their great guilt and fear from religious beliefs or the influence of old learning patterns. This is true with sexuality, religion, parent-child relationships and husband-wife psychology. Many of my female clients experience this predicament – conflict among religious, cultural and parental upbringing, which are totally opposite their current priorities and preferences. Mental programs and memories should be upgraded and updated in order to resolve these conflicts.

Memorized information is powerful data for the concrete mind and common sense. The faster and better you can memorize, the more data upon which to base decisions and deductions. The only problem is: What kind of data are you using? There is a saying, "Garbage in, garbage out". That's the danger, so we should be selective in what we read, learn and put into our memory. This includes visuals and input from TV, news, books, audio and video references.

This learning process affects children, teenagers and adults today. They sometimes pick up the wrong social models, TV programs and music selections. This is also the danger of fast memorization techniques used in speed reading. The wrong information quickly mentally photographed in the past might be stored without discrimination or a process of reason. The materials and information that feed our senses and memory should be screened properly. There is such a thing as mental energy diet and proper mental nutrition.

How to Make Decisions and Solve Problems Using Your Mind

The design of the concrete mental faculty is to construct ideas, deduce and process details and organize them in the mind. This is expressed as the ability to use details and particulars in the general scheme of things.

When a person's mental energy field is bright, calm and strong, the organizing and concretizing ability of the mind is efficient. Therefore, the mental thoughtforms and goals in life are clear and strongly vitalized, especially if the mind is equipped with sufficient information related to the project or subject.

Best results are achieved when ideas, goals, procedures and schedules are properly and clearly written. It's often better to rewrite them several times until everything is simplified, clear and organized. You may notice that before you started writing, you assumed you already knew everything clearly. But the moment you try to write your ideas and goals on paper, you pause periodically and change the sentence, then sometimes cross the statement out. It means that you are not as clear yet on what you really want, or your mind has not organized it yet. So writing your thoughts and ideas helps you clarify, improve and organize them.

FAST PROBLEM-SOLVING TECHNIQUE

In problem-solving and decision-making, for example, the mind works best when you write the following:

1. What is the real issue or problem?
2. Is it real or a by-product of fear or reactive emotions?
3. Who is involved and affected by the problem?
4. How much time do I have to solve it?
5. Who can help me, and what are the necessary talents or aptitudes required of them?
6. How much money (if required) is involved to solve the problem, and what is the source of funds?
7. What are the probable solutions? Select and analyze more than two possibilities. What are the benefits and consequences of each solution?
8. After using your mental evaluation, countercheck with your emotional and physical instincts to determine the best solutions and decisions. Ask for an expert's opinion, if required. Integrate solutions for win-win outcomes. Use role-reversal to test fairness to people involved.
9. List the best solution, procedure, budget and personnel, if needed.
10. Make the complete schedule and final plan, including contingency plans for potential obstacles.

Once you write and evaluate everything, mental confusion is minimized and the overwhelming effect of emotional reactions is reduced or eliminated. Writing things and organizing them on paper exposes the erroneous blind spots and unforeseen obstacles. It also shifts you from the negative side effects of emotionalism into a more mentally intelligent approach to managing crises or creating plans. This is the next step for masses of humanity to employ the mind to solve its world problems.

How Your Mind Researches, Investigates and Analyzes

The concrete mind has the faculty of comparing duality and the power to analyze interrelationships of data and information. By continuous focus, data-gathering and investigation of deeper and broader implications, applications and details, the mind will be able to penetrate the greater reality of forms, just like drilling down into the nature of the physical body – from the general structure to the organs, tissues, cells, atoms, molecules and sub-molecular particles. Then the next step in investigation goes beyond the physical form to the world of invisible energy.

This search and investigation using the concrete mind is well demonstrated by the modern scientist, Harlow Shapley, the first person to measure the size of the Milky Way Galaxy as 300,000 light years across.[6] He claimed that the Milky Way Galaxy was the cosmic whole. The story of this great scientist was challenged by the new discoveries of Edwin Hubble, a famous astronomer who used the 100-inch/25.4-centimeter long Hooker telescope at the Mount Wilson Observatory. He discovered that the universe extends beyond the edges of the Milky Way Galaxy and in 1929, he further concluded that the universe was expanding.[7]

This discovery eliminated Einstein's uncertainty about his general theory of relativity. Earlier astronomers assured Einstein that the universe was neither expanding nor contracting. These conclusions affected his earlier equations, but by the sheer power of timing, the potential blunders in his equations were resolved by Hubble's discoveries into what we know as Einstein's equation of relativity.[8] So, you see, the concrete mind power of research and investigation can lead to great unfoldment of valuable tools and equations, but those who don't use the mental faculty properly or validate theories with other methods can be victims of wrong and incomplete mental evaluation. Thus, the power of the mind is like a double-edged sword.

HOW YOU CAN USE A UNIVERSAL MODEL TO CONCRETIZE YOUR IDEAS

If you observe and study how ideas, technology or science are physicalized into objective reality as products and services, the general patterns used are as follows:

1. First, the idea is known.
2. The idea is studied and categorized into principles.
3. The principles are organized and categorized into processes and procedures.
4. The processes and procedures are subdivided and categorized into methods and techniques.
5. The methods and techniques are categorized and organized into steps.
6. The steps are either qualified, quantified or timed.
7. The whole system and technology are manufactured, priced, packaged and sold.
8. Marketing, continued research and product development ensure innovation, improvement and new designs in technology, products or services.

The above process displays how the concretizing power of the concrete mind works, creates and innovates. Looking at successful organizations and pioneering technology, what power do you think fueled these great achievements? Many great minds have pooled their concretizing mental powers to make the endeavor a success. Successful organizations or endeavors are not like mushrooms growing overnight. They are a by-product of tremendous mental power and effort.

The power of the concrete mind can also be used in many ways to organize and concretize your life's goals and manage your time properly:

7 STEPS TO PLAN YOUR LIFE AND MANAGE YOUR TIME EFFECTIVELY

1. Think of the most important areas of your life that you need to satisfy and fulfill.
2. Identify the most important vision, mission, plans and goals that you need to achieve short-, medium- and long-term.
3. Identify and properly design the most important roles corresponding to the mission/goals you have set for yourself.
4. Knowing your roles and goals, identify the most important activity and job description for you to perform in all the chosen areas of your life.
5. Knowing the most important activities to complete monthly, weekly and daily, design the most important events and results you need to implement, qualitatively and quantitatively.
6. Create a schedule in your calendar or planner to list and organize all the details.
7. Implement schedules with discipline.

The most important initial step in organizing your life and managing your time properly is to know exactly what you want to do in life and what you want to achieve. This is summarized in your vision and mission, which will become a plan.

The vision, mission and plans of our lives
are the lighthouse, compass and map
we need to reach the shores of success
and the land of fulfillment.

Organizing and planning our lives and managing our time wisely do not only depend on how disciplined we are about putting deadlines in our planners or calendars. It is more than just writing, following and beating deadlines. The schedules and results should constantly follow a path of coherence with life's purpose.

Our true time and life management
revolve around priorities based on our
noble vision, practical mission and realistic plans.

11 Steps to Concretize Your Vision and Goals

For those who want to use the mind systematically and technically, you can maximize performance and success by employing it to organize and implement your projects and goals:

1. First, define the goals, project objectives and end results.
2. Determine and classify the general activities.
3. Subdivide the activities into tasks, functions or roles.
4. Break down the tasks into work or job descriptions.
5. Establish a scope of work and results to be achieved, with their quality, quantity and schedule.
6. Determine the financial and material resources and their sources.
7. For group projects, determine and organize the implementers and workforce with the top leaders as a priority. Once they are chosen, they can help with the details of organizing. Make sure the personnel expenses can be covered in the financial budget, otherwise adjust the plan.
8. Determine possible problems and obstacles. Make a contingency plan for potential problems ahead of time. Avoid surprises.
9. Create the final schedules with deadlines, follow-up dates and a list of implementers and targets.

10. Regularly monitor and evaluate the plan, situation and project development. Adjust the plan as required.
11. Always know the greatest benefits and service of achieving your goals. This will inspire you to make the required sacrifices.

If you observe the sequence of this concretizing technique, it involves a flow from generals to particulars. Most great projects and goals are physicalized with the power of the mind and constant focus. When I started to write this book, I had already seen and organized the general contents and chapters in my mind, with the whole outline from beginning to end. I had already imagined the flow of ideas. I knew what I needed to write, and I just started to write all the words and ideas, letting them flow according to the pre-determined goal of the book.

No matter how sharp your mind, it can still be honed to become even sharper and more brilliant. There is no end to its training and usefulness. That's why many corporations are investing a lot more in the proper training of their workforce, especially the management. The new system of upgrading the workforce includes mental training to think of new ways to create, not just to follow orders or manage linear models of business execution. I wish that more corporations would realize that the true investment and assets in the organization are the people and that the real, tangible assets are the quality of people in the workforce and the mental powers of their leadership.

> *Technology depreciates easily,*
> *but people can appreciate for higher-value investments*
> *with proper mental training.*

I believe that the real job of an executive, professional and especially a leader is to be the real thinker and mental powerhouse of the organization.

DO YOU WANT TO PAVE A DIRT ROAD OR BUILD A SUPERHIGHWAY?
The Difference Between Innovation and Creativity

What's the difference between innovation and creativity? It is best expressed in this statement:

Innovation is converting the dirt road into blacktop while creativity is constructing a new superhighway.

While innovation is employed in revising, adding, subtracting and converting old things into new, better forms and features, creativity is a new idea that dramatically changes an old idea or creates a new feature or form altogether. We can see some basic examples in the improvements in the design and features of some familiar products or technology:

1. CAR MANUFACTURE:

Innovation:
- Add an off-road 4-wheel drive feature to 2-wheel drive vehicle for snow and muddy road applications
- Convert a 4-cylinder pickup to an 8-cyclinder truck for more power

Creativity:
- Add cup holders to front and back passenger areas in a car. This may be one of the single most creative additions to cars in several years. Why didn't anyone in the automobile industry think of these creative yet inexpensive features earlier? The smart person who thought of cup holders used their creative powers to create a new concept.
- Minivans and SUVs to meet specific family needs not addressed by traditional cars or trucks

2. LASER POINTERS:

Innovation:
  -Improving the old plastic pointer for teaching into a stainless steel collapsible pointer

Creativity:
  -Inventing the laser pointer (pioneering)

Innovation:
  -After a few years, laser pointers were improved with the addition of lines and different highlight shapes in the original laser pointer (an improvement).

3. RAZOR BLADES:

Innovation:
  -Improving the traditional one-sided razor blade to double-sided razor blade for shaving

Creativity:
  -Invention of single-blade disposable razors (pioneering new idea)

Innovation:
  -Improving the single razor into 2- and 3-blade types

Creativity:
  -Inventing waxing and laser systems for hair removal

4. PROJECTORS:

Innovation:
  -Making the transparency projector collapsible into a lighter, small hand-carry size and improving the lamp brightness

Creativity:
  -Inventing the LCD or video beam projector that projects an electronic document from a computer (pioneering)

Innovation:
  -Improving the LCD into a lighter and smaller size with a remote control and easy hook-up

5. ROCKETS:

Creativity:
-According to the writings of Jeffery Kluger[9], Dr. Robert Goddard invented the first supersonic and multi-stage rocket with fin-guided steering in 1935.

Innovation:
-German scientists visiting, investigating and inspecting Goddard's rocket before the war developed their allegedly copied V-2 missile bombers used during World War II.

Innovation uses concrete mental powers to revise, rectify or convert old things to better forms and improvement. It still involves the concrete mind and partially the abstract mind when there is a dramatic change of concept. Creativity is not revision or just mere addition. It is not just an artistic faculty. It is a new pioneering principle, concept, idea or activity.

Walt Disney exemplifies creativity. According to Richard Schickel, Walt Disney, the founder and powerful creator behind the Walt Disney entertainment world who conceived Mickey Mouse, the first talking cartoon (1928); Snow White, the first full-length animated film (1937); Disneyland (1955) and Epcot (1964), created sensational breakthroughs and pioneering work in the entertainment and movie industries.[10] The greatness of his personal growth came from his decision to flee from home at the age of 16 after a difficult childhood of poverty to become one of the world's most influential animation pioneers of our time.

> **KNOW YOURSELF:**
> Are you more creative or innovative?
>
> | | Yes | No |
> |---|---|---|
> | I am known as a pioneer and I like to bring breakthroughs (creative). | ____ | ____ |
> | When I hear of an unmet need, I am able to create a new solution (creative). | ____ | ____ |
> | I prefer to improve on pioneering or existing ideas, solutions or products. (innovative). | ____ | ____ |

If your abstract and concrete mind are activated, integrated and employed to discover and create new tools for the evolution of life, greatness can be achieved and success is predictable. The stories of the lives of successful personalities and celebrities in this book are employed as case studies to further elucidate the principles of success and fulfillment and how they used their minds in their achievements. The stories do not imply that I approve or disapprove of their lifestyle or personal issues.

Creativity is best expressed by this statement:

Do not go where a path may lead you,
go instead where there is no path and leave a trail.
Ralph Waldo Emerson, American poet, philosopher and essayist

THE CURE FOR BOREDOM:
Use The Power of Your Imagination

The creativity of the abstract mind is never complete without mentioning the power of imagination. I usually call it "creative imagination". There are two types of creative imagination: imagination of the mundane and imagination of higher creative ideas towards the future. Most children and "spacey" adults enjoy the first type, which we call daydreaming. This may lead a person to get out-of-body and experience inner travel to another plane. It is usually the imagination of the normal world. It is like your experience while sleeping.

The real power of imagination is the second type, which many great artists and some abstract writers use. The realm of imagination is a frequency or state of consciousness in the abstract mental world where ideas and futuristic concepts are found. That's what one of our abstract-minded artists meant in the statement:

> *The man who never in his mind of thoughts*
> *travel'd to heaven is no artist.[11]*
>
> William Blake, English poet

When a person's abstract mind is already active, it can connect easily to the Earth's abstract realm through meditation, creative imagination or sleep when people get out-of-body. The Earth's abstract dimension contains the world of ideas and principles not usually known to the concrete mind. When your mind is refined, playful and not rigid, it is easy to tap into this higher realm.

What is the difference between visualization and imagination? They are both apparatus of the mind, but visualization is a faculty of the concrete mind and imagination is the faculty of the abstract mind. That's why creative artists are more mentally fluid compared to most engineers, whose minds are more fixed and objective. Innovation primarily utilizes visualization and creativity uses imagination more.

Let's study several examples of these two faculties:

Visualization Versus Imagination
EXAMPLE 1

1. You can visualize your fingers because you have seen them before. This process uses the concrete mind.
2. You have to imagine how to clap with only one hand because you have not seen that at all. The concrete mind ceases to function in imagination, and the abstract mind starts to be stimulated.

EXAMPLE 2

1. Visualize your childhood: What were your favorite toys? This technique involves the concrete mind because you travel to your known past.
2. Imagine your life 10 years from now: What will you be wearing and what will you look like? This mental process utilizes the abstract mind and creative imagination to imagine the future.

Normal events and occurrences stimulate the concrete mind, and extraordinary concepts stimulate the abstract mind through imagination. Here's another example:

EXAMPLE 3

1. Visualize that you are relaxing in bed and reading a book. This is so obvious and normal that the concrete mind visualizes it easily.
2. Imagine that you are a point of light relaxing inside a tetrahedron. This process involves the abstract mind for most people.

A tetrahedron cannot be visualized if it has never been seen, and most people have never experienced imagining their body reduced to a small point of light.

When the concrete mind is too rigid as with some adults, they can hardly imagine unknown things. Children are more imaginative because their mind is still flexible. If you tell children to imagine becoming a point of light, they can do it easily, but ask an adult to do it, and many won't even dare close their eyes to experiment whether it is possible. The concrete mind immediately blocks the possibilities without even attempting to use the creative imagination.

An imaginative person is more creative, more futuristic and has greater potential to materialize bigger realities. Very concrete-minded people with poor imagination usually limit their mind to thinking of smaller possibilities, thus they end up with lesser probabilities resulting in a smaller reality.

On the other hand, a person whose abstract mind is more developed has a better faculty of imagination and generally entertains bigger possibilities, resulting in a better probability and ending up in greater realities.

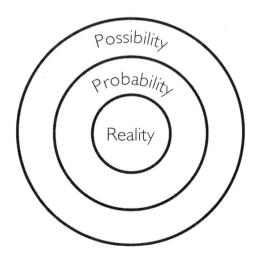

The diameter of each day is measured by the stretch of thought —
not by the rising and setting of the sun.

Henry Ward Beecher, American minister and author

Advanced abstract thinkers are usually more forward-thinking and dynamically positive because their mind allows their imagination to see ahead to greater possibilities that have never been explored before or can even be opposite common sense. This is one of the big contributions of the film industry, always showing humanity what lies ahead. Before cellular phones and electronic watches were made public, James Bond films were the advance promoters. Before Neil Armstrong and other astronauts landed on the moon, the movies portrayed stories of outer space exploration.

Movies give examples of creativity and the power of imagination. They show the current impossibilities that shape human beings' future possibilities. Once human minds can visualize a result through imagination, a person can eventually do what they imagine and visualize. But the effect of the movie industry is like a double-edged sword. It can cut in both positive and negative directions with visions of the future: evolutionary or involutionary.

Why is the process of imagination important for one's success and fulfillment?

- Because it is a tool of creativity and allows one to conceive new ideas.
- Because it develops the abstract mind to advance its powers to tap into the future. Then you can become a visionary.
- Creative imagination precedes the development of the intuitional faculty. This explains why more artists and mystics develop the intuitive faculty faster than concrete-minded scientists.
- Creative imagination is the faculty that brings a sense of humor. Humor is a by-product of creativity and a wild imagination.

When scientists learn how to use their imagination, not only visualization, great discoveries will result in the unthinkable!

When 3 minds meet and cooperate —
the concrete mind of the scientists,
the creative imagination of the artists
and the guiding principles of the philosopher —
the future world will be a super-world!

Entertain life's possibilities beyond what the concrete mind can fathom using your imagination. This will keep you moving to the future with greater visions and reality — to the world unknown to most people. Think like an artist. If you are an artist, create works of art never seen by people before, and bring human consciousness forward to the future. Paint or write from the future, and your work will be the lighthouse of new frontiers.

People with mental creative powers are always ahead. They are the pioneers, and they lead humanity to new adventures and breakthroughs. These divine co-creators from the ranks of humanity are the pillars of every country's structure and the directing compass towards the future.

The power of this mental creativity, like creative inventions or discoveries, is truly pioneering, but the new ideas are sustained and born from the knowledge of the past. Inventors and pioneers utilize and incorporate the wisdom and experience of the previous generations as a building block. Even Einstein credited Edwin Hubble's discoveries of the expanding universe with making him adjust some factors in his famous equation of relativity.

Computers and the Internet came about thanks to the previous invention of electricity, electrical components and communications technology. The invention of electricity was made possible because of the invention of metals. The discovery of more refined and advanced types of metals and compounds innovated electrical systems into electronics, and then the computer came about. Without an electricity source, today's computer is nothing, as you may have experienced when your laptop computer battery dies. Even Microsoft would not shine without PC hardware.

All the so-called technology pioneers can't create or innovate without these earlier creative discoveries and inventions. Without the creative pioneers of metal production, even the international air, water and land travel we enjoy today would not be available to us. So every inventor or discoverer of new technologies and sciences should maintain humility and have a sense of gratitude towards the creators and innovators of science and technology in each past generation. What we call modern science and technology are the by-products of the power of the mind of many civilizations.

Close your eyes and imagine for a few seconds how it would be if we removed all things produced for us by business, science and technology creators. Where would we be? Start with your body, your home, car, city. Close your eyes and imagine if we did not have scientific innovations and inventions. What do you see? Today, could we handle the situation for a month?

ENJOY THE *Abstract Mind* OF EINSTEIN AND THE *Concrete Mind* OF NEWTON WITH MOTHER TERESA'S *Heart*

Love-intellect is one of the last faculties of your mind to be mastered because it involves the development of both your concrete and abstract mind, augmented by the sensitivity of your heart.

There are two power centers that activate and regulate the mental faculties:

- ◆ Throat power center: Concrete thinking faculty
- ◆ Mid-brow power center: Abstract thinking faculty

Your mental aura or mind is made up of thought substance and vibrates at a higher frequency than your vitality and emotional auras. It also integrates and extends beyond these auras. By activating your throat and mid-brow centers, your mental functions and powers are awakened further. To make this more effective, it is advisable to first purify the mental substances of negative thoughts, intentions or thought patterns obstructing your mind from growing. After that, we will activate and revitalize your throat and mind-brow centers through breathing techniques. To integrate and balance your concrete and abstract mind, we will simultaneously focus on them and do the inner breathing. Your heart center will also be stimulated to sensitize emotional intelligence and compassion to safeguard the use of your mental powers only for good purposes; thus, a new faculty and inner power will evolve into the love-intellect faculty. This technique is required to develop the power of focus and awareness.

Practical Techniques
TO BECOME A MENTAL POWERHOUSE

The mind needs mental exercise to grow.

There are many strategies to apply your creative intelligence and mental powers for greater success and fulfillment. Many great thinkers and leaders have already mastered some of these methods. These methods are for those seeking ready-to-use guidelines.

THE MENTAL POWER OF FOCUS AND AWARENESS
Inner Purification of Your Emotions and Mind
(7 minutes, twice weekly)

1. Sit in a comfortable position with your spine vertical and your feet flat on the floor. Close your eyes to enhance the concentration.

2. Visualize you are in front of the ocean and breathe slowly and deeply. Relax (30 seconds).

3. While breathing slowly and deeply, mentally intend to breathe out and expel all stress, tension and negative feelings to the ocean, especially during exhalation. Imagine that the ocean is absorbing them. Just relax (2 minutes).

4. Continue the breathing technique and intend to breathe out and expel all negative thoughts, intentions, confusion, mental disturbances and any harmful thoughts against yourself or others. Imagine that the ocean is absorbing all of these (2 minutes).

Revitalization and Activation
of Your Mental and Emotional Faculties

1. Concentrate on your heart center and breathe slowly and deeply (10 times).

2. Concentrate on your throat center and breathe slowly and deeply (10 times).

3. Concentrate on your mid-brow center in between your eyebrows and breathe slowly and deeply (10 times).

4. Simultaneously concentrate on the mid-brow, throat and heart centers and breathe slowly and deeply (10 times).

5. Mentally say the following affirmation 7 times:

I am a creative and intelligent person.
I will use my creativity and intelligence lovingly and properly.

6. Practice this technique after a shower or bath and before eating full meals. It may not necessarily be safe for smokers and people with heart conditions to practice this technique. If you are not certain, consult your physician before you start.

METHOD TO DEVELOP FOCUS AND AWARENESS:
Breathing Technique to Develop Your Love-Intellect Faculty

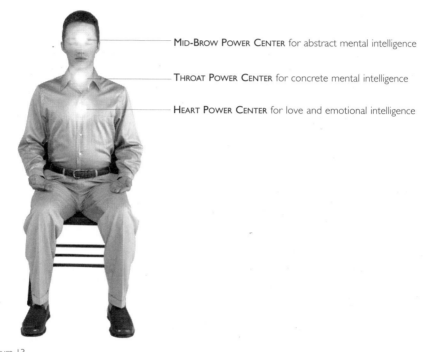

MID-BROW POWER CENTER for abstract mental intelligence

THROAT POWER CENTER for concrete mental intelligence

HEART POWER CENTER for love and emotional intelligence

Figure 13

For a more advanced method to develop the love-intellect virtue and the faculty of focus-awareness, use the following technique.

Rapid Love-Intellect Faculty Development (4 minutes, twice weekly)

1. Do the Synchronized Breathing Method (3 sets of 10 breathing repetitions). This is for fast energy purification of the vitality, emotional and mental auras.
2. In between sets, simultaneously focus on the mid-brow, throat and heart centers while breathing slowly and deeply for 30 seconds.

   Note: The rapid love-intellect faculty development is an alternative technique to the first method for focus and awareness.

It is not recommended for pregnant women or for people with neck or spine issues or migraine. If in doubt about your condition, consult your physician before using the technique.

If you do these emotional-mental faculty development techniques regularly twice a week, expect a notable change in your thinking capabilities, with more integrated concrete and abstract mental faculties and emotional intelligence. This quality is the next goal for human development: the good qualities of an Albert Einstein, Sir Isaac Newton and Mother Teresa all in one personality. How about that?

KNOW YOURSELF:
Do you have the love-intellect faculty?

	Yes	No
I actively seek out and surround myself with smart, experienced people.	___	___
I am able to explain abstract principles with concrete examples and metaphors.	___	___
I am able to extract a principle from a series of concrete facts.	___	___
I implement ideas and goals that are win-win as much as possible.	___	___
I use my heart to assess concrete situations and abstract philosophies.	___	___
I am good at adhering to long-term vision and can manage daily details with the sensitivity to adapt to change.	___	___

If you answered "yes" to most of the questions,
then you may already have developed the love-intellect faculty.

WHAT KIND OF THINKER ARE YOU?

In addition to developing your concrete and abstract mental faculties combined with emotional intelligence, it can be helpful to know that there are three groups of thinking styles:

1. People who are too focused, meticulous and like details
2. People who are too general and like principles and philosophies
3. More advanced thinkers who are both naturally focused and aware, an integration of the above two natures

Detailed Thinkers

The first group, the detailed and concrete thinkers, tends to have an active and big throat power center and more left-brain activity. They are very good at concentration and concretizing projects, and you can rely on them with specifics. They tend to be more accurate and scientific. Day-to-day affairs is the name of their game. The problem is that they are usually lost in details, sometimes forgetting the general plan and long-term goals. They tend to be telescopic in perception and scrutinize others' faults through a microscope. The seed of failure in this group is the emotions, which are not necessarily developed or are under-stimulated and thus, have atrophied. Usually, these people seem relatively cold and indifferent. They tend to be introverts or enjoy working alone. But they are good focused implementers. They usually finish what they start. They tend to be subordinates or researchers, or they are not the center of the business. If you are not this type of person and your boss is an extremely concrete type, it can be difficult. Typical philosophers, artists and mystics are the opposite of this personality because they hate details and rigid structures. Both groups can learn from each other's style through osmosis or interaction.

The Philosopher Type

The second group is the philosophers and some artist types. They are good at generalities, principles and creative abstractions. They are not as pragmatic as their detail-oriented counterparts, say the engineers, lawyers and accountants. They usually like to discuss ideas for a long time, but act on them slowly. These people are more abstract thinkers, and the mid-brow center is more active than the throat center.

You can encounter both types of thinkers in a business meeting: The results-oriented people bring a thick file of data and graphs into the meeting, talk immediately about results and ask the bottom line, and the abstract thinkers bring a thinner file and maybe a book with quotations marked to remind you of the principles of success. These people are also always aware of the vision statement and general long-term plans. The more abstract-minded group usually checks and balances the quality of processes in an organization. They see longer-term implications of the company's role in the future. They are practitioners of awareness and sensitivity and are the visionaries.

Integrated Thinkers

A third type of thinker is a person who integrates focus and awareness.

> *When the concrete mind,*
> *abstract mind and heart are active and integrated in a person,*
> *he or she is the best of the best leaders or thinkers.*

Integrated people are motivators, inspirers and transformers, yet have very good acumen in managing personnel, resources and investments. They are more advanced people whose long ancient experience has endowed them with love-intellect integration. Most of these great thinkers specialize not only in the what's and how's of things, but also the why's. The incoming generations of top thinkers will express this integrated faculty. When the educational systems catch up on the emphasis of inner practical values, plus the training of the abstract mind in the curriculum, lessening and simplifying the learning process of the concrete mind, the mass development of real geniuses — heart-mind thinkers and leaders — will be common everywhere.

KNOW YOURSELF:
What type of thinker are you?

	Yes	No
1. I don't make decisions without facts and data.		
2. I am good with details.		
3. I like to go straight to the bottom line on any decisions.		
4. I am very focused when I work.		
5. I creatively imagine scenarios and outcomes when making decisions and solving problems.		
6. I base decisions on long-term vision, strategies and goals.		
7. I rely on principles more than details to make decisions and solve problems.		
8. I consider how a decision can violate and affect universal principles.		
9. I am known as both a motivator and a technical manager.		
10. I easily integrate the generals and particulars of most situations.		
11. I understand the causes behind events and am able to concretize solutions.		
12. I decide based on an integrated combination of research, data and options guided by principles.		

If you answered "yes" to questions
1-4 you are probably more of a detailed thinker.
If you answered "yes" to questions
5-8 you are probably more of a philosophical thinker.
If you answered "yes" to questions
9-12 you are probably more of an integrated thinker.

12 STEPS TO CREATE A LEGENDARY LIFE AND FIND YOUR NICHE
Strategies to Deepen Your Life's Purpose and Mission

One of the most potent uses of your mind is to deepen your life's purpose and mission. Many clients have come to me for coaching because they sense they have a bigger purpose in life, but they don't always know how to identify or implement it. Here's a technique to do this for yourself:

1. **DETERMINE YOUR POINT OF INTEREST WHERE YOU ALREADY HAVE A GOOD MENTAL GRASP OR SUBSTANTIAL EXPERIENCE.**

   Is it in the field of leadership, politics, psychology, education, philosophy, business, diplomacy, arts and music, culture, physical sciences, healthcare, technology, religion, social and human sciences, metaphysical sciences, energy sciences? Select one or two fields.

2. **USE AN INTEGRATION OF EMOTIONAL AND MENTAL FACULTIES AND INSTINCTS TO SEARCH FOR NEW IDEAS RELATED TO YOUR SELECTED FIELD(S).**

   What ideas? Ideas that solve the common pervading complex problems of humanity and the world. Start with the concerns, issues or needs observed in your family, neighborhood and workplace. What do people you interact with complain about: a product, a service, an issue that has not been resolved or for which no business or organization has a solution? Write all of these answers down, and compile and gather information about these needs lacking attention or a supply of solutions.

> *Great creative ideas and pioneering inventions*
> *come to humanity not because we merely want them,*
> *but because we need them.*
> *They come first to people who can access them*
> *because of high aspirations to help serve humanity*
> *and add more meaning to the world.*

3. **NURTURE THE IDEA OF HELPING EVOLVE OR SOLVE SOMETHING EVERY DAY.**

   This can be a missing niche or link in the chosen field in which you have great interest, knowledge or experience.

   Never forget the value of a big idea. In our case,
   a single big idea can add $600 million to $700 million
   in sales in one year.

   John Martin, President and CEO, Taco Bell[12]

4. **IDENTIFY WHERE YOU CAN INNOVATE OR CREATE.**

   Once you have felt in your heart and conceived in your mind that there is an area of specialization or subject where you can deploy some expertise, you can be sure that things exist to be discovered. For example, why do new and even better companies constantly emerge and succeed in the computer industry even though there are so many experts already?

   IBM was once admired and feared as the dominant player in the computer industry. Then Microsoft came along to dominate the PC market with Bill Gates' ability to innovate existing functionality. But Steve Jobs, considered a master of hardware, software and creative graphic arts and co-founder of the Macintosh computer and Apple in the 1970s, is a leader in this industry – not a follower, not an innovator but a creator – despite Apple's ups and downs. Then there's Larry Ellison, founder of Oracle and database king.

   There are many more examples: young Yahoo billionaire founders, Jerry Yang and David Filo, who created a great Web directory powerhouse and Scott McNealy of Sun Microsystems, who introduced the user-friendly Java open programming language.[13] I'm sure the computer and Internet industries have not been saturated yet. There will always be one or more great creative-minded people who have the power to innovate and create new avenues of products and services that will be even better than the existing ones. With the above examples, I endeavor to present the idea of great possibilities, new niches and untapped potentials for many people. Select an area of expertise or interest, then find or discover the missing untapped potential idea/product/service that you can embark on to develop.

5. **MAKE THIS NEW IDEA PART OF YOUR PURPOSE AND MISSION IN LIFE.**
    Create an aspiration of serving or wanting to serve, not only yourself, family or organization, but dedicate and surrender this project for the service of humanity and planetary evolution. This process is important because it opens your heart and top-of-head power centers and the spiritual connection that brings the real inner powers in you to make this happen, the power of the higher aspects of yourself. This naturally brings inspiration for you to proceed and build momentum.

    The initial impetus has to have breakthrough force and strong inspiration because when you start to physicalize a project, a lot of demoralizing conditions usually arise to squelch your desire to continue. Especially with big ideas, you need a big boost of patient persistence to drive you forward. Look at the space shuttle: The maximum required thrust and fuel is during the initial stages of the flight. Once the momentum is set, your continued interest and aspiration will be your lubricant to go forward, allowing you to finish what you start.

6. **OBSERVE THE POWER OF SILENCE FOR SOME TIME UNTIL YOU ARE READY TO ACT.**
    Do not divulge your ideas, vision and plans unnecessarily to other people until these are solidified, especially to people who are not positive, supportive or trusting of you. Even some friends and family members who do not understand your higher purpose and mission should not be informed prematurely. When people criticize or negate your plans, it weakens the plans and slows you down. It also creates doubts

in you that can weaken your interest in your new ventures. Even your thoughts can be read or sensed by your peers, associates or people closest to you. Beware of jealous people. People can steal your idea or ruin it prematurely. Of course, in an established team or department in a corporation, it's a little bit different. You need to feel your way to tell the right thing to the right person or leader at the right time.

7. **CREATE A BALANCED RESOURCE GROUP AND TEAM.**
    If you want to be the original proponent and leader of this project or idea, after you are sure and prepared to reveal your vision and plans, create a balanced resource group who can help you with more detailed and accurate data-gathering and fact-finding. You don't have to divulge the whole thing until you are sure of your team members. Reveal just enough for them to work properly as a team. If you choose to have only a limited partner for this project, choose the best person to work with. Proceed with caution, but with certainty of success. Choosing your right co-workers aligned to your purpose and mission is the primary key to success.

8. **PROCEED AND GO DEEPER INTO YOUR MENTAL WORK.**
    Continue penetrating all avenues and possibilities that can make your chosen project or field a unique, extremely powerful and much-needed breakthrough. Do not spread your mission or idea too thin or in too many directions. This will not bring you focus unless you already have a big organization supporting your cause. For every additional goal or strategy, there is a tremendous increase in requirements for resources and manpower. Go for minimum resources and maximum output in the shortest timeframe guided by the right timing.

9. **GO DEEP AND NOT TOO WIDE!**
    New projects tend to fail when the initiator and their team are too ambitious, trying to cover everything in order to con-

trol the whole process without selecting specializations. Every increase in the scope of a plan requires a tremendous amount of energy and personnel and exponentially increases the period to accomplish it. It is better to dig a hole 1 mile/1.61 kilometers deep and 3 feet/.9 meters in diameter than 1 mile/1.61 kilometers in diameter and an 1/8-inch/.3175 centimeters deep.

For a pioneering breakthrough, there should generally be a selected niche or line of specialization. How did great pioneers and creators become globally known experts? Most of them were proponents of only one selected idea, specific equation or element. For example:

a. Marie Curie became significantly important because of a discovery she worked on for most of her life: the discovery and unleashing of the power of radium and radioactivity. I'd like to add a complementary principle here that we discussed earlier as the process of conceiving new ideas due to humanity's need. Her discovery of radium and radioactivity came about right before World War 1. Luck and the power of timing made her project and services particularly necessary at that time for the soldiers since x-ray machines could locate shrapnel in their bodies. Thus the need for her service and related inventions at a particular time was brought about by their usefulness.

b. Einstein's reputation and pioneering work are summarized by the $E=MC^2$ equation, which made him extremely famous. He was known for a specific area of expertise, and he dug a deep hole a few feet in diameter.

10. **KNOW YOUR BRAND AND STICK TO IT.**

What is your summarized slogan and the motto of your project or area of expertise? There should be a few powerful words summarizing your new work or creation. By putting the underlying purpose and meaning of your new mission or specialization into one succinct statement or a concise slogan, the power of the vision and mission increases. This is the power and magical use of words. The slogan and motto of your new work or emblem are the reminders of your new purpose.

When you design a logo, create a very important symbol that summarizes the project. Once you put your logo and mission statement-slogan into final artwork, the project becomes even more empowered. I call this "baptism of the organization", after which it really becomes an energetic entity. The logo and slogan affect the destiny of the mission to a great extent, so choose them properly. When people see you and your logo, it is your brand, symbol and an energetic summary of your project or mission.

11. **CONTINUE THE INTELLIGENT DISCIPLINED WORK.**

Do not lose sight of the original purpose and mission. It is easy to be sidetracked along the way. Patient persistence is required of all pioneering work because you are the one digging and shoveling the soil and rocky ground for the first time to open a new road towards the future.

Do not compromise your inner values and noble purpose whatever happens along the way. It is not just the end results that are important, but also how you manage the process to achieve them. Sacrificing inner values and compromising virtues can create serious negative consequences, so it can be better to achieve slower and more spiritually clean success than to risk compromising values for false results. In almost every pioneering work, there is a degree of resistance from the populace or environment and from competitors.

PATIENT PERSISTENCE AND COURAGE ARE NEEDED FOR PIONEERING WORK: *The Rachel Carson Story*

Let's look at what happened to a pioneering American environmentalist, Rachael Carson, as related by Peter Matthiessen.[14] Rachel Carson wrote the famous book, *Silent Spring*, in 1962, which was a compilation of her scientific research, investigation and findings on the negative and poisonous effects of chemical pesticides on the natural environment. Her patient persistence and clear vision of her purpose to help save the natural environment bravely pushed her against the violent intimidation and threats of lawsuits by big corporations. Also, before she became a well-known author, her literary works were said to have been rejected by 15 magazines, including *Saturday Evening Post* and *National Geographic*. So we can see the persistent, single-handed effort and force she employed to finish the goals set before her. Later her works were published and heralded as a body of environmental service. If there are obstacles that challenge your creative path to unleash new services and breakthroughs, just remember this woman born in 1907 who was a brave environmentalist before environmentalism as a movement existed.

12. POWER OF SACRIFICE:

The power of our achievement is directly proportional to the levels of our sacrifice in life.

If you think your newly chosen creative mission will have an end result and influence on evolution greater than your life, it is worth a sacrifice of most things in your life in order to leave a legacy. This principle has always served as a guiding light for the lives of great leaders, great Saints, Sages and world servers. What do we usually sacrifice? Lesser things for bigger goals: time, effort and our personal preferences.

Every worthwhile accomplishment has a price tag attached to it. The question is always whether you are willing to pay the price to attain it — in hard work, sacrifice, patience, faith and endurance.

John Maxwell, American leadership expert

This strategy applying the powers of the mind for the creation of new, important and sometimes extraordinary projects and services will allow us to become extremely useful in society.

Businesspeople, scientists, educators, politicians and more mentally-developed people will benefit from this above strategy because it offers some potentially useful hints and techniques to help already-great achievers perform even better and more efficiently. It also serves as study material to periodically experiment with to move to your next purpose and mission in life.

Now that you have learned ways to deepen your life's purpose and mission and find your niche, let's explore some techniques to materialize your goals properly.

PROGRAMMING AND MATERIALIZING YOUR GOALS PROPERLY
Visualization of End Results with Safety Program

Visualize the positive and happy outcomes and positive end results of your goals and plans, including the good effects for you and the people concerned. Mentally program your results by making strong intentions, wishes or visualizations that the goal will physicalize only if it is good for your whole life; if not, it should not happen. Mentally programming your positive goals needs repeated concentration and visualization to make it powerful.

5-Step Programming and Materializing Technique

1. See your goals with mental clarity and focus on the positive end result.
2. Mentally see your goals already accomplished and visualize only the positive successful outcomes.
3. Have high expectation and strong conviction that the goal will succeed.
4. Be committed to the positive goals and end results.
5. Work on your "luck". Good karma + intelligent disciplined work

Guidelines for Programming and Materializing Your Goals

1. *Set your goals with mental clarity and focus on the positive end results.*
   This is the first important step without which the other steps have minimal power. Very successful people and achievers are masters of this first step. Despite obstacles, they achieve their goals because from start to finish, they are very clear about what they want. Indecisiveness is a vice. Make sure the goal is in accordance with your life's vision and purpose and is aligned to your good principles. Once the goal is set, the next step is to maintain focus and constancy.

2. *See your positive successful outcomes already done successfully and visualize only the end results repeatedly, not the process of achieving them.* The more you concentrate on the end result, the stronger it becomes.

3. *Have high expectation and strong conviction that your goal will happen successfully.* This step creates strong enthusiasm and energy for the goal. Avoid doubts.

4. *Be committed to the positive goals and end results.*
    Commitment is very important. All the above steps will not yield the speed and power of materialization without real commitment. Commitment is the power that drives you to finish the goal with determination and constancy of effort. Part of commitment is the creation and implementation of schedules and deadlines. This is the backbone for your end results.

THE POWER OF KNOWING YOUR GOALS CLEARLY:
The Sam Walton Story

Sam Walton, the founder of Wal-Mart, one of the most successful businesses in the US during his time, is a great example of the power of goal-setting. When he started to envision Wal-Mart's strategies in his mind, he probably committed to being the best in his line of business. He was determined to adapt the best processes of retail stores and innovate them to be better and to bring the lowest prices to smaller US cities.

According to John Huey, who wrote about Sam Walton in the *Time* 100 Magazine, "In 1985, Forbes magazine determined that his 39% ownership of Wal-Mart's stock made him the richest man in America[15]". When Sam Walton died in 1992, with a family net worth approaching $25 billion, he left behind a broad and important legacy in American business, as well as a corporate movement. As Huey recounts, "In 1998, Wal-Mart was the No. 4 company in the *Fortune* 500, behind only General Motors, Ford and Exxon, with annual sales close to $120 billon[16]".

Wal-Mart's Board of Directors and staff (and Sam Walton before he died) are always clear on Wal-Mart's main goal, enumerated in their slogan: WE SELL FOR LESS ALWAYS. This focus is what makes them very successful.

If you know the positive end result and constantly focus on it, maintaining physical, emotional and mental commitment to it, almost nothing can stop you from accomplishing it. It's just a matter of time.

5.   *Work on your luck: Good karma + intelligent disciplined work*

Luck chooses those who work for it.

What does this statement mean? If we combine the good grace of entitlement called good karma with intelligent disciplined work, we can achieve almost any goal. Good karma has two forms, current and ancient.

a. Entitlement and good karma in this life: Many people start at the bottom but today are at the top of their chosen careers. Oprah Winfrey, a television personality in the United States, is an example. According to an article written by Deborah Tannen, she started out as a simple girl with no special lineage. Born on January 29, 1954 into a poor family, she amassed an estimated personal fortune of more than $500 million by the time she was 44[17]. I believe that her generosity and her philanthropic works supporting educational funds to send disadvantaged kids to college, as well as much unpublicized charity work, have given her the grace of good luck (in addition to her hard work and ability to invest properly). As Deborah Tannen went on to write, "Winfrey stands as a beacon, not only in the worlds of media and entertainment but in the larger realms of public discourse[18]".

A Christian teaching says:

God is not mocked:
For whatever a man soweth, that shall he also reap.
Galatians 6:7, The Bible

This universal law is also mentioned in most religions, including Islam, Buddhism, Hinduism and Judaism.

b. Ancient endowment: If religions believe that what you plant today, you will harvest in the future, planting and harvesting must have an interval period and process. Many believe in rebirth; others don't. The question is: How do we explain why some people have an easier time and effort, amass wealth and get what they need without working very hard for it? Some people are not mentally gifted, were not born into a fortunate lineage and are not necessarily spiritual, but they suddenly become instant millionaires by winning the jackpot lottery.

I think there must be an ancient source of invisible wealth endowment. Is it a coincidence, or is there a perfect spiritual karmic mathematics, which looks for people who worked before (maybe in ancient lives) for what they are abundantly receiving now? These people most probably were generous and benevolent personalities who helped many people in their ancient past; now is the time they are entitled to and are harvesting their luck.

Intelligent disciplined work is another aspect of luck. Disciplined work guided by proper organization, time management and creativity, lubricated by good karma or entitlement to receive, is a major aspect of materializing our goals rapidly and properly. Hard work is not enough. Many people are hard-working, but not successful.

I am a great believer in luck,
and I find that the harder I work,
the more I have of it.

Thomas Jefferson, Early President of the United States

Herein lies the significant difference between "mentally-polarized" people and emotionally-reactive people. Mental personalities are usually more structured whereas more emotional people tend to be more impractical and unfocused. Many successful leaders and achievers have done so well and have materialized their goals so effectively because of proper short-, medium- and long-term preparation. This expresses itself as the right timing of events, good investments and good outcomes of decisions, which make a person, organization or country appear lucky. But the success of prosperous or developed countries or organizations did not happen overnight. They worked hard, sacrificed and prepared for the next harvest of abundance and success.

Intelligent disciplined work is a product of a well-organized, well-informed and disciplined mind. In this epoch of our civilization, we can predict that the countries and cultures that continually evolve faculties and powers of the mind will stay ahead in politics, education, business, arts, sciences, technology, culture and spiritual development, especially if these nations and peoples maintain goodwill, will-to-do-good, compassion and generosity — in other words, the powers of their heart. They will be unbeatable, and they will serve as the ideal model of future culture — a scientific culture guided by love and wisdom. This will be the result of using mental powers for greater service and for the advancement of humanity and the world.

The empires of the future will be the empires of the mind.
Winston Churchill, British Prime Minister

Now that you know the basic differences and functions of the concrete and abstract mind, we can proceed to the practical strategy to stimulate or fertilize the abstract mental powers.

How to Train Your Abstract Mind

The highest faculty of the mind is abstract mental power, which is related to the use and formulation of higher ideas, principles and philosophies.

Here are ways to enhance and culture it.

1. ### Investigate the why's.

    As much as possible, investigate the "why's" or purpose of things, events, uncommon knowledge, existence and life. If you keep on answering the why's, you enter into the realm of principles and concepts, which in the long run leads to universal ideas and laws. Then you are in the mental frequency of the abstract world.

    Withdraw periodically from routines and repeated activities. With redundant activity and events, the abstract mind is not exercised because it is your physical instincts and concrete mind that are employed daily. Look for new assignments or add activities to your schedule that are unfamiliar to deprogram the rut in your mental functions and execution.

2. ### Study new discoveries

    Study new and advanced technological and scientific discoveries and ask yourself, what are the new principles and concepts behind them? Look for the creative and innovative ideas involved and study them as universal principles and subjective laws. For example, the invention of the TV, radio and cellular phone can be interpreted as a divine manifestation of Omnipresence on the physical level. The Internet now used globally and packed with huge libraries of information can represent the abstract idea of divine Omniscience. The nuclear or atomic bomb can also be seen abstractly as a crude material expression of the Omnipotence of creation. There are new discoveries concerning procreation and artificial reproduction through in vitro fertilization and the production of tissues from stem cells that can be interpreted as humanity evolving to become a physical creator. So with the cloning of animals and species — these are physicalized powers of the human mind primarily using the abstract mind to guide the concrete mind to physicalize so-called spectacular inventions. The above abstract mental practices train one to understand and relate concrete discoveries to universal principles.

Reading or hearing about important political or financial events in the news, you can try to penetrate the underlying causes and effects, especially the hidden meaning of those events. A real thinker knows a lot more than common sense and trains him- or herself not to be a human parrot. When people employ this practical continuous method of mental training, starting from childhood to the post-graduate education level, we will experience a generational leap of consciousness from the mundane mediocre focus on trivial events to deep understanding of the world of causes. Most thinking processes have evaluated world events only at the surface level, always blaming somebody for one's sufferings or mistakes. Once the abstract mental principles are unfolded, the search for solutions, missing gaps and links for the meaning of our existence will be directed from external to internal. Then the real truth and causes will be understood. World history will be an important teacher, and wars may be avoided. True world peace and unity will be an inevitable result.

3. *Study works of poets, artists and philosophers.*
    Study poetry, quotes and literary works from great philosophers, Sages and writers like Lao Tzu, Shakespeare, Tagore, Rumi, Helen Keller and other excellent artists. Here is an example of poetry illustrating an advanced abstraction of the mind:

> *To see a World in a Grain of Sand*
> *And a Heaven in a Wild Flower*
> *Hold Infinity in the palm of your hand*
> *And Eternity in an hour.[19]*
>
> William Blake, English poet

Penetrate the underlying principle and universal values and concepts in their poems, quotes or literary works. Many of these writers experienced advanced abstractions of material life and understood some inner cause and underlying reality that can explain mysteries and inner experiences. Once you realize and understand life's subjective principles, the abstract mind is exercised and fertilized. That explains why the more advanced modern scientists like Albert Einstein, Edwin Hubble, Thomas Edison, Sir Isaac Newton and Marie Curie were not just utilizing their concrete mind, but were also able to connect with universal principles and concepts through their abstract mental faculties.

If you study the movie industry, some of the script writers and directors are geniuses in their own right, producing and directing what they consider works of arts and creativity, but which actually involve the use of concrete and abstract mental faculties. A good example is the Wachowski brothers, who wrote and directed "The Matrix", an interesting abstract movie.

4. *Employ introspection.*

In problem-solving, experience a different strategy from the usual emotional reaction and instinctual solutions. Try to understand the problem first by asking:

a. What is the lesson behind the problem for me and the people concerned? What was the violated virtue or principle? Why has it happened?

b. What are the adjustments I need to make to avoid it happening again?

c. What are the principles and values gained if I solve it, and how do I apply them immediately? Realizing the principle and concept without making a repair is not complete. Learn by avoiding the mistake and resolving to correct the situation, if required.

d. Take a few hours of silence every week undisturbed by anyone just to create new ideas or think about abstract principles and concepts that are forward-looking or futuristic. If you are the leader, always be the one who has more advanced and futuristic ideas and information than others.

Respect for leaders often comes from the fact
that people naturally respect those
who know more than they do.
That is one of the jobs of a powerful thinker,
to be thinking ahead where no one has gone before.

You can use some weekly questions to improve your work and performance in life guaranteeing continued success:

♦ What new principles and ideas can produce extraordinary improvement in my ability to deliver results in support of my goals and service? Above-average thinkers should do at least one hour of pure thinking training weekly. Super-achievers or leaders of leaders should do at least two hours per week.

Beware of the barrenness of an overcrowded life.
Anonymous

- What is the future of this business, project or role? What concepts, principles or ideas do I need to employ for explosive growth?
- Review and internalize your life's vision, mission and plans more deeply. There are always hidden meanings and untouched depths of your life's purpose. Unleash and unfold them in a more refined, noble and cultured way.

5.   Focus on breakthroughs.

Always focus on breakthroughs or innovations that humanity needs and which have not been seen before.

Vision, determination and hard work are not always enough. Failure sometimes means simply that others do not share your dreams. Commit yourself to work that contributes to the social good —
and commit yourself with equal energy to the society closest to home, your family. Education is a lifetime pursuit. Success requires the constant acquisition of knowledge and skills to compete in a world of accelerated change.
Charles E. Young, Chancellor, UCLA[20]

6.   Go beyond your normal truth.

Always search for even greater awareness of the purpose of your life and higher existence by asking, Who am I? What can I be? Sometimes we need to start from zero, or from what the Zen teachers call emptiness, to really search for the right answers. As we search for deeper universal truths, we can partially connect to Macrocosmic purpose using the abstract mind. This process is like opening a spiritual antenna for higher reception of ideas.

Your mind is an excellent tool, not only for greater success, but also for sustained fulfillment. It's a great idea to use your mind regularly and enjoy sharpening it. It is better equipment than any technology to organize your daily life continuously, harvest the lessons of the past, accurately forecast the future, make good decisions, solve problems properly, innovate our world and create a new culture. You can name unlimited applications.

Scientists have maximized use of their concrete minds, the philosophers their abstract minds. And hopefully your mind has evolved just by reading this section of the book. Isn't it said that knowledge is power? Therefore, by increasing the amount of positive information in your mind, you are no longer the same. This is accurately portrayed by this famous statement:

> *One's mind, once stretched by a new idea,*
> *never regains its original dimension.*
>
> Oliver Wendell Holmes, American author, poet and physician

Our continuous learning is always the sign that we are alive and evolving, and we can be sure that with patient persistence, we will grow towards the light that illuminates our whole being, allowing us to be the guiding lights for others. And we will become the light for the dark corners of the world. It's just a matter of time before the mind can be mastered. It has already begun. But the pursuit of all the needed knowledge and learning takes a lifetime. According to a Chinese proverb:

> *Tell me, and I will forget.*
> *Show me, and I will remember.*
> *Involve me, and I will understand.*
>
> Confucius, Chinese philosopher

KNOW YOURSELF: Rate your level of mental development. Rate 0 to 4.	DEVELOP YOURSELF: Check the top 3 mental faculties you want to focus on improving in the next 6 months.
Common sense	Common sense
High grade of common sense ____	High grade of common sense ____
Memorizing and storing information ____	Memorizing and storing information
Mental analysis ____	Mental analysis ____
Problem-solving and decision- making ability ____	Problem-solving and decision- making ability ____
Capacity to materialize goals ____	Capacity to materialize goals ____
Ability to organize and structure ____	Ability to organize and structure ____
Innovation ____	Innovation ____
Creativity ____	Creativity ____
Ability to visualize ____	Ability to visualize ____
Imagination ____	Imagination
Love-intellect faculty/ focus and awareness ____	Love-intellect faculty/ focus and awareness ____
Legendary vision and knowing your niche ____	Legendary vision and knowing your niche ____
Philosophical and principle-based thinking ____	Philosophical and principle-based thinking ____

In this chapter, we've shown how the mind works, its uses, functions, faculties and applications and how to develop mental faculties rapidly and properly for many of your life's strategies. Apply and practice the techniques so that you will "understand" through your own personal experience the path to become a legend and a mental powerhouse beyond what you have already achieved.

When your mind is honed as a powerful integrated tool, regulated by the conscience of your heart and the force of your will-power and vitality to initiate action and finish what you start, you are on the road to total success and fulfillment.

The synthesized three qualities of will-power, love and creative intelligence can bring maximized performance and a balanced life. But for success to really last and transform into fulfillment, there is one more important element — the eight core values that can help you:

- Identify and overcome your blind spots
- Avoid mistakes
- Be entitled to bigger results in life with certainty
- Bring a deeper meaning and purpose to all you do
- Balance your material and spiritual life and accomplishments

When you successfully balance the five most important areas (Family and Home, Career and Work, Health and Recreation, Social Life and Environmental Contribution, Spiritual Life), integrate the three qualities of the Success and Fulfillment Triangle and apply the eight core values, you can get what you want, enjoy what you have and do more than most people can achieve in a lifetime.

CHAPTER 7

8 CORE VALUES
TO BALANCE YOUR
MATERIAL AND SPIRITUAL LIFE

A key to transforming success into fulfillment is a daily life guided by values or spiritual virtues. These virtues are like gateways or portals to develop inner, noble faculties and present great opportunities that can create lasting fulfillment and a more balanced material and spiritual life. Let's study how the virtues work and get developed faster to facilitate the path from success to fulfillment.

MASTER YOURSELF THROUGH THE POWER OF VIRTUES

Your personal powers of success can only be harnessed safely and used for greater good if your personal character is cultured with virtues and inner values. In terms of safety, we are not only talking about the harmful effects of a person's attitude towards others, but also about the danger of hurting one's growth and end results if one's character is not cultured.

There are several virtues and inner values to be mastered to be able to handle and sustain big achievements properly and to create avenues where you can go to the next great step of self-fulfillment. A reciprocal relationship exists between virtues and faculties. The process of applying a virtue is a faculty. The faculty is an instrument to express virtues and inner values. Each virtue developed corresponds to inner powers acquired and levels of spiritual development attained. The more the virtues are mastered, the greater your power to succeed and be fulfilled. Let's study the subject of virtues and put them into practical application. The following are virtues and corresponding benefits when they are mastered:

8 KEY VIRTUES TO MASTER YOUR LIFE

1. *Discipline and Constancy:*
   The key to attaining great achievement constantly
2. *Will-power and Vitality:*
   The key to speed and continuity of long-lasting performance
3. *Objectivity and Practicality:*
   Power of discrimination to achieve balanced results — the antidote to fanaticism
4. *Benevolence:*
   The power to achieve happiness, contentment and right human relations and the key to accessing greater powers safely
5. *Altruism:*
   The key and power behind prosperity and sustained abundance
6. *Group consciousness:*
   The key to sustaining power and achieving bigger goals in less time
7. *Virtue of Sacrifice:*
   The key to greatness and powerful service and the power to become a legend
8. *Good health:*
   The key to attaining and enjoying lasting success and fulfillment

Let's discuss each of these virtues and their benefits in detail.

The Discipline and Constancy Virtue is a Must to Become a Super-Achiever
The key to attaining great achievement constantly

When one has discipline and constancy, success is predictable!

This virtue is the mark of a champion in the Olympics, business, spirituality or any of life's endeavors. Our case study of Oscar Wayne training for the Olympics is a good example of cultivating the discipline and constancy virtue.

Why are some people more successful? Why have they achieved more in less time? Not just because of talent, because many talented people have failed repeatedly in history, nor is it only technological advancement because many scientific and technology experts also fail. It is the discipline and constancy of focus accompanied by constancy of effort that are the most important factors propelling people to attain great achievements constantly, any time they want them. The virtues taught by most religions and spiritual schools emphasize the aspects of love, compassion, generosity and truthfulness, yet seldom do they emphasize the practical aspects of virtues and values.

On the other hand, competitive sports, martial arts and military training have always embodied this virtue, which produces the best athletes in the Olympics, the most skillful martial artists and the most decorated soldiers. Due to the force of competition for excellence and future promises of financial reward, university students also develop this virtue, which scientists and businesspeople later master throughout their careers.

The people who have mastered the virtue of discipline and constancy become super-achievers. To practice true discipline and constancy the following are recommended:

10 STEPS TO BUILD THE VIRTUE OF DISCIPLINE AND CONSTANCY

1. *Set your goals clearly and implement them properly.*
   Set your targets and goals clearly and know by heart your most important roles and end results. Make sure that your goals are important and form a good part of your life's vision. It is not enough to be constant in effort if the direction and purpose of the goal to be accomplished are not positive, certain or clear. Know your goals and required results, qualitatively and quantitatively, by writing them until you are clear and definite about them. Constantly focusing on them in good and even bad times is the key to discipline. Remind yourself of your goals and results in your calendar or planner and use reminders throughout your house or work place. Put them into a slogan or motto. An organization or team can do the same.

2. *Go extra miles in effort and time.*
   Mastery of any work or endeavor needs more time than normal and the force of disciplined will. In general, the thing that you have done the best is what you put more time, energy, resources and effort into with constancy and unwavering focus.

   The most successful people are those who
   are able to go the extra mile in effort and spend more time
   doing the most important things
   that bring the greater value to life.

3. *Write your strategy and schedule on paper.*
   Write a practical strategy and schedule that specifies the exact dates and time needed to accomplish the goals, and accommodate the activity that produces the required results.

Follow the schedule and deadlines you set for yourself strictly without compromise. Writing and knowing the schedules and results are not enough to be disciplined. You need to implement strategies and monitor your results. Adjust accordingly based on your periodic evaluation.

4. Make a habit of finishing what you start.

Finish what you start as much as possible. For most achievers and successful people, this is already a habit, but under-achievers need to work more on this aspect. You can start on smaller and short-term goals and projects that inspire you to get into the habit of finishing what you start. If you have done this several times successfully with smaller targets, then achieving larger goals becomes less and less difficult.

5. Focus on results guided by virtues.

Focus on the results, but do not compromise virtues in implementing the process. Sometimes people sacrifice the processes and procedures just to achieve what they want, even to the extent of violating virtues. It is counterproductive in the end, just like athletes who take steroids to enhance their performance in the Olympic Games, but end up losing it all when their medals are revoked. Or some businesspeople and politicians who achieve their goals in the short run, but experience bigger failure later on. (Study the case of Enron for a clear example of this.) Real discipline takes into account the right virtue and process to achieve the best results. Do not forget that your goals are just steps to long-term plans, and it is not the end of the world for you if you do not achieve them. After you do your best, be detached to whatever results follow and accept them. It is your attitude, after all, that matters.

6. Succeed and be alive.

Work to achieve best results in the shortest time, but make sure you survive. Successful winners or champions are more useful healthy and alive than sick or dead. Do not sacrifice your health or life just for one goal you set. You are not the goal. It is just one of the targets you have created. The goal is not you. You have more things to achieve than one goal. Therefore, avoid being excessive and causing great discomfort to yourself or others or loss of life in pursuit of goals.

> *One should not mistakenly interchange*
> *courage and foolish fanaticism. These might be similar qualities,*
> *but they are not the same attitude.*

7. *Have a contingency plan and avoid surprises.*
   List all attitudes and obstacles that negate your goals and results, and work them out. Plan contingencies to solve anticipated problems and avoid surprises. Develop the next skills, aptitudes and attitudes needed for your next steps or goals. The MDP Life Planner (available at www.mdpglobal.com) includes self-assessments and forms to help you do this.

8. *Handle adversity properly.*
   Discipline is best tested and developed where there is a critic or the presence of competition. Therefore, implement goals with a sense of urgency. If confronted with competition, approach it in a detached, balanced way.

9. *Get a qualified coach-mentor.*
   Do not rely on your own natural capabilities. For important goals, get a coach or mentor who has been there, a wiser person or an expert. Select your coach or mentor based on their track record.

10. *Be creatively adaptable.*
    Change or adjust your goals and targets if they are destructive or counterproductive to your life.

Developing the discipline and constancy virtue is easy through energy science, so let's explore some methods.

Advanced Energy Method to Enhance the Virtue of Discipline and Constancy Faster

People's attitudes and aptitudes are externalized results and manifestations of the conditions of the person's aura and power centers. By knowing the different power centers responsible for discipline and constancy, we can activate them to express the virtues.

The following power centers enhance the virtue of discipline and constancy:

- **Base-of-spine:** Physical stamina, strength and practical groundedness
- **Navel:** Vitality, staying power and instincts
- **Solar plexus:** Determination and emotional commitment
- **Heart:** Emotional stability and inner peace
- **Mid-brow:** Mental stamina and will-power
- **Top-of-head:** Wisdom, spiritual will-power and detachment

2-Step Method to Improve the Virtue of Discipline and Constancy (2 times weekly)

1. Do the **Synchronized Breathing Method** (5 minutes).
2. Focus on the following power centers while inhaling and exhaling slowly. Hold your breath for a few seconds in between inhalations and exhalation. Do 10 slow breathings for each power center as follows:

    - Top-of-head
    - Mid-brow
    - Heart
    - Solar plexus (8 times only)
    - Navel (Avoid this step if you are pregnant.)
    - Base-of-spine (Omit this step if you have cancer, high blood pressure or are pregnant.)

In these modern times when life's pace is so fast and the demands and challenges are more complex, mastering the virtue of discipline and constancy is a great advantage. This is a virtue that makes great leaders, successful businesspeople, extraordinary athletes, brilliant scientists, Saints and Sages excel in whatever endeavors and goals they embody. Not all of the above groups have mastered benevolence, but all of them have discipline and constancy of focus and effort to be successful.

Your Will-Power and Vitality Are What Keep You Going Faster and Farther
The key to speed and continuity of long-lasting performance

Many people perform great miracles with the virtues of benevolence and altruism; others do well creatively with the virtue of objectivity and practicality, but without will-power and vitality, it is not easy to maintain performance at a greater speed and to continuously sustain effectiveness in life. Without will-power and vitality, it is impossible to master the virtue of discipline and constancy, it is difficult to overcome difficulties and obstacles and people tend to preserve the present and dwell on the obsolescence of the past. This is one of the main challenges of Estella Walsh, our teacher case study.

> *Will-power pulls people out of the past*
> *and pushes them to the future.*

With will-power and vitality, benevolence and altruism can be expressed naturally and continually. When people are low on vitality and will-power, it is difficult to be effective in life. It is also not easy to be pleasant when you have a low battery.

Will-power and vitality are best expressed as follows:

- Vitality is the fuel for greater performance.
- Will-power is the 4-wheel drive to boost the power of performance and effectiveness in life. It is the dynamite that allows you to blast through great obstacles and difficulties.
- Will-power is the pioneering force that opens and constructs your road to success where others have not gone before.

> *The speed achieving your results and the levels and quality of your success are directly proportional to the levels of your vitality and force of your will-power.*

How many people get so frustrated because they fail in the last stage of their projects due to the lack of power at the end? Many people usually start strong and enthusiastic, but their will-power runs short and vitality drops before finishing projects. What makes great champions and winners is not just the starting phase of the game, but the end game. This is true in chess and in sports. It is also true in business performance and personal relationships. The winning edge and the ability to achieve great goals require extraordinary vitality and sustained will-power.

TECHNIQUES TO IMPROVE YOUR WILL-POWER

You learned many techniques earlier in chapter 4 for vitality management. Here are some methods to improve your will-power. Choose any method that suits you.

A. **EXERCISE AND INNER BREATHING METHOD** (3 times weekly):
1. Internal Stamina Exercise: You can refer to pages 76-86 in chapter 4 or follow the available DVD.
2. Breathing techniques to boost vitality (choose either of the techniques):

    ◆ 5-10 Abdominal Breathing Method: pages 92-93
    ◆ Combination Breathing: pages 94-95

B. **SQUATS METHOD** (2 sets a day, 3 times weekly):
  1. Expanding squats exercise (20-30 squats): page 78

C. **BODY SQUEEZE METHOD** (3 sets, 3 times weekly):
  1. Synchronized Breathing Technique (3 sets)
  2. Body squeeze procedure (3 sets): Do this while standing straight with your hands at your side and feet together. This method involves inhaling fully and holding your breath for 7 seconds. Then squeeze all parts of your body to increase vitality and will-power. After the total squeeze, exhale slowly and relax for 20 seconds. While holding your breath, the lungs and blood absorb more oxygen. More spiritual energy also comes in as a result of inhaling and holding your breath. If you want to lose weight in particular parts of your body, you can focus on squeezing these parts more than others.

D. **PUSHING AND PULLING EXERCISE** (3 sets, 3 times weekly):
  1. Synchronized Breathing Technique (3 sets)
  2. Pushing and pulling procedure (3 sets):
    a. Stand with your feet apart at shoulder width.
    b. Shake your body continuously in rhythm, loosen up and decongest blocked areas and parts (3 minutes).
    c. Maintain the position of your feet, but bend your knees into a stance as though you were riding a horse.
    d. Put your hands with palms open and facing forward at chest level.
    e. Inhale deeply and fully and hold your breath for a few seconds.
    f. While holding your breath, push your palms forward until they are fully extended directly out in front of your chest. As you are pushing your arms tensely, squeeze your entire body and exert force as if you were pushing a car. After

full extension of your arms and breathing out all your air slowly, relax your whole body while your arms are in an extended position. Breathe slowly for 10 seconds.

g. With your arms fully extended in front of you, breathe deeply and fully and hold your breath for a few seconds.

h. Squeeze your entire body and pull your hands as if you were pulling a car towards you. Finish pulling when your palms are back in their original position.

i. Exhale slowly and relax your whole body with your hands at chest level with palms open and facing forward. Breathe slowly for 10 seconds.

j. Repeat steps e-i 2 more times.

The first time, do only 2 sets of pushing and pulling. It is a very intense exercise that boosts your vitality and will-power fast.

Note: The following people should not practice the body squeeze and pushing and pulling exercise will-power development techniques:

- High blood pressure patients
- Glaucoma patients
- Pregnant women
- People with heart conditions or chest pain
- Migraine or headache sufferers
- People with hernia
- People with arterial problems
- Unhealthy elderly people or anyone over 50
- People with high stress
- Smokers, alcoholics and drug addicts
- People with cancer or AIDS
- Epilepsy and vertigo patients

Consult your physician before you try this method if you are in doubt about your condition.

E.   POWER CENTER BREATHING TECHNIQUE (10 min, 2 times weekly):

1. Do the Synchronized Breathing Method (3 sets for 3 minutes).
2. Do power center breathing as follows:
   a. Focus on your **mid-brow, navel** and **base-of-spine** power centers simultaneously while breathing slowly for 2 minutes. Use only the mid-brow and navel power centers if you have high blood pressure or cancer or are pregnant.
   b. Focus on the **heart, mid-brow** and **top-of-head** power centers while breathing slowly for 2 minutes. Use only the mid-brow and top-of-head power centers if you have heart conditions.
   c. Absorb and store energy in your navel area by focusing on your **navel** power center while breathing slowly for 3 minutes. This is an important step to absorb internal power that sustains vitality and will-power.

Developing will-power takes more time than increasing vitality. Almost anyone can boost vitality quickly, but not always will-power. Will-power depends on the development of certain power centers like the mid-brow, top-of-head, navel, solar plexus and base-of-spine.

People born in poorer countries where manual labor and struggle are an everyday part of life develop more physical stamina and will-power. People from richer countries develop their physical and mental will-power through sports, military training or business management requiring great will to overcome organizational adversities.

Children born to poorer families usually have more avenues at an earlier stage to develop their will-power than those from richer families who live more comfortably. Developed countries where life is more comfortable and people live in abundance tend to be weaker in the lower aspects of will-power because people do not get exposed to daily difficulties and struggles. I would not be surprised if nations with maximum comfort and minimal stretch of will-power will be challenged with some future national difficulties to balance their development and increase their will-power faculties.

The virtue of will-power and vitality is necessary to improve performance and quality of life. It accelerates the speed with which goals are achieved. It also helps a person move towards the future with greater productivity and effectiveness. It is a necessary power that leaders, parents and groups need in order to fulfill their roles and goals. Will-power and vitality are the marks of a true long-lasting leader.

Your Virtue of Objectivity and Practicality is Your Indispensible Tool for Success
Power of discrimination to achieve balanced results – the antidote to fanaticism

We are finishing an era during which the martyr complex is common in individuals and groups, and fanaticism through excessive idealism and blind faith are the guiding attitudes of many leaders and their followers. It is a dangerous world where excessively fanatical sects and militant groups are busy implementing their religious or nationalistic ideals.

How did this come about? What is the antidote to this fanaticism and excessive idealism? There must be a flaw in certain educational processes or some religious teachings that triggers the lack of objectivity and practicality in many people.

The virtue of objectivity and practicality develops the power to know and perceive the truth properly and the ability to adapt a method or action that is suitable and appropriate to the situation. It is an attitude of being realistic and grounded.

How Can You Develop the Virtue of Objectivity and Practicality?

As there are many levels of truth, you need different levels of faculties to perceive truth and information. Then after concluding the facts properly, act upon and use them properly. Perceiving truth accurately is the first step, and expressing the truth or information in a practical manner is the second step. Many brilliant people research information and conclude the facts, but do not use the data for practical application. What a waste of time and data! On the other hand, many practical people perceive the right information, but due to lack of wisdom, express the data wrong and destructively. Both accurate and objective perception are musts, and practical application is required.

10-Step Method to Master Your Higher Perception

1. *Use your gut instincts.*
   If there are insufficient data in a very urgent situation, use your physical gut instincts. This requires the development and instinctive powers of the **navel** and **base-of-spine** power centers.

2. *Feel situations with your emotional gut feelings.*
   If you have developed emotional instincts, use your emotional gut feeling to validate the rightness of the perceived data, information or situation. Most people use the **solar plexus** for this, not the **heart**, and are biased in some situations. Using the emotinoal instincts of the heart brings the conscience of right and wrong and win-win decision-making.

3. *Discern with your heart.*
   Use your emotional intelligence or inner conscience to sense what is right. This is a function of the **heart** center.

4. *Discriminate using your concrete mental reasoning.*
   The concrete mental intelligence for analysis has to be used properly to discriminate what is right and wrong and what is ideal or practical. Verify all the above findings from steps 1, 2

and 3 using the process of concrete reason. The **throat** power center is employed for this faculty.

5. *Use your common sense to validate ideas properly.*
   Evaluate all the above findings by comparing them to existing common sense. This is the function of the **throat** center and the concrete mind. Scientific data are still the most reliable sources of common sense. Be careful with common sense because it has its own limitations and obsolescence.

6. *Understand situations through principles and philosophies.*
   Since not all advanced information and events are known through common sense, evaluate the situation or data employing the abstract mind. This requires abstract principles and philosophies to validate the information. The questions, "why"? and "what for"?, are used to probe deeper into the issue or situation. The **mid-brow** power center and the abstract mind are utilized for this faculty.

7. *Employ the faculty of intuition.*
   For more advanced people who have partially developed the faculty of intuition or have sufficient intuitive awareness, perceive the idea or situation and sense if it is coherent with bigger universal ideas. Evaluate if it lends a sense of integration with greater truth.
   The **top-of-head, forehead** and **mid-brow** power centers are required to develop this faculty, with the help of the Soul's wisdom. This faculty, considered an advanced subjective tool for most people, is included here to accommodate more advanced human beings who have partially developed intuition. In the distant future, advanced humanity will have this faculty as part of its natural abilities.

8. *Test the universality of the idea and information.*
   Another tool to evaluate the objectivity of data or informa-

tion concerning philosophy is to test the universality of the idea or information. How inclusive and encompassing is it? Does it foster separativeness, or does it improve synthesis or coherence with a greater truth? Do the data violate the interpretation of holy scriptures or universal teachings? Consider the knowledge and presentation of truth from the spiritual sciences or from the teachings of the Eastern Wisdom. This is not necessarily connected to the so-called "New Age" interpretation and information. Be wise and selective in choosing references.

9. *Consult experts on the subject matter.*
   If you are still doubtful at the end of all these tests and evaluations of truth, consult an expert on the subject matter. If you are still uncertain, get a second or third opinion from other experts.

10. *Synthesize information and ideas.*
    At the end, synthesize all the gathered data and opinions and decide according to the best discriminating faculty you have developed.

This whole process might seem tedious at first, but when you practice this protocol, especially by briefly writing the evaluations, you will develop the power of real objectivity. The more you use the different levels of validating truth, the more secure and certain you are in your discrimination and perception.

GUIDELINES FOR DIGESTING INFORMATION AND EXPRESSING PRACTICALITY

1. In general, it is not necessary to look for the absolute truth in an idea or information, but to evaluate what components of the data are correct, acceptable or not valid. This is where

people have difficulty because they are either perfectionists or too idealistic. Sometimes you need to be patient like a miner finding the gold or diamond in a mountain. The same is true with great ideas or information: We need to look patiently for the precious part of the idea or data. Know the limitation and percentage of probability and potentiality of the truth, idea or concluded information:

a. What percent of it is possible? What are all the possibilities?

b. What percent of it is probable? What are all the probabilities?

c. What are the limitations and potentials?

d. What elements can be wrong? What aspects are valid?

e. What are the seeds of success of the idea or situation?

f. What are the seeds of failure of the idea or situation?

g. What can go wrong? What are the potential problems?

h. What are the worst things that can happen? Can they be handled safely or properly?

i. What are the positive and negative effects on others and the environment?

j. Does the perceived information or situation support or negate universal values and higher principles in life?

2. Express the perceived truth, idea or situation in many practical ways that benefit you and others. Write the answers to the following:

a. What are the potential ways to use these data, information, truth or situation? Choose the best ways to use the truths or situation.

b. What are the benefits for others?

c. What are the positive and negative consequences?

d. How many are benefited and to what degree?

e. How long will the positive or negative effects last?

f. How do I start to use and apply this data? What are the strategies?

    g. What are the contingencies and probable solutions for any foreseen obstacles or problems?

    h. Create a short-, medium- or long-term plan based on the questions and information above.

    i. Study and apply procedures from chapter 6 on problem-solving (page 137), concretizing ideas (pages 139-142), visualization of end results with safety program (page 167) and 5-step programming and materializing technique (page 168).

    j. Synthesize all your best answers and devise a practical plan to apply the right information, data or situation. Select one or more practical ways that can benefit your life and improve the lives of others. Make sure you will finish what you start with the highest-quality results and a sense of urgency. These guidelines are specially designed for bigger and more complicated situations or for more complex fact-finding endeavors.

    k. After implementing your decision, monitor results and summarize them in a report.

You Can Apply the Objectivity and Practicality Virtue Immediately

In general for daily simple situations, practice applying objectivity and practicality with the following method:

1. Briefly relax and center yourself for a minute, if stressed. Use the Synchronized Breathing Method; even 3 sets will suffice.

2. Use your physical and emotional instincts to perceive information or a situation fast.

3. Evaluate the perceived data using your common sense and concrete reasoning faculties. Check if the data or part of the information sound right.

4. Check the data or situation to see if they are good for your life and for others.

5. If the situation is good and beneficial, go ahead and apply it immediately. If it is destructive and harmful, forget it and drop it immediately.
6. Make sure it is in line with your life's important goals and is not only beneficial for the present, but also for the long term.

Objectivity and practicality is a necessary virtue to produce great outcomes in life, and it is the key to avoiding wrong decisions and preventing fanaticism. Being benevolent, altruistic, actively creative and intelligently grounded to do the right actions creates balance in life.

ENERGY METHOD TO DEVELOP THE VIRTUE OF OBJECTIVITY AND PRACTICALITY (7 minutes, 3 times weekly)

1. Do 3 sets of the **Synchronized Breathing Method** for 3 minutes. Do not do this if you are pregnant or suffering from heart conditions, high blood pressure or migraine.
2. Focus on your **mid-brow, navel** and **base-of-spine centers** while breathing slowly for about 2 minutes. For people with hypertension or who are pregnant, only focus on the mid-brow and navel centers.
3. Focus on your **mid-brow, throat** and **heart centers** while breathing slowly for 2 minutes. This will develop both emotional conscience and an integrated concrete and abstract mental faculty.

This technique is simple, but it helps you develop the virtue of objectivity and sense of practicality guided by conscience if practiced regularly.

Discrimination can be used synonymously for objectivity if wisdom is added to this virtue. A good example of this advanced objective virtue is the Buddha, who was a master of discrimination and wisdom. The following statement is an exercise of discrimination.

We must not believe in a thing said merely because it is said;
nor traditions because they have been handed down from antiquity;
nor rumors, or such; nor writing from sages, because sages wrote them;
nor fancies that we may suspect to have been inspired by a deva
[angel]; *nor inferences drawn from haphazard assumptions we may have*
made; nor because of authority of our teachers or masters. But we are
to believe when the writing or doctrine or saying is corroborated by our
own reason and consciousness. For this I taught you not to believe
merely because you have heard, but when you believe of your
consciousness, then act accordingly and abundantly.

Lord Buddha, the Enlightened One

Some mystical and religious groups and idealistic people may want to incorporate the virtue of objectivity and practicality in their daily decision-making and problem-solving. Mystical people are very good at emotionally and intuitively perceiving the truth. In fact, many of them are psychics and visionaries who recognize situations or information ahead of others. But they need to enhance the sense of practicality in using the information and the ability to react properly and in a timely manner to the events. The lower power centers, especially the navel and base-of-spine centers, have to be activated and revitalized for more practicality and groundedness. Idealists should act upon their ideas and ideals immediately and make these ideas useful in many ways. Talking and preaching about the goodness and greatness of ideals is not enough. Walking the talk is more important.

One good idea applied immediately is better than
five ideas memorized and stored unused in the mind.

Businesspeople are good at practicality and scientists are good at objectivity. The economist, Adam Smith, was precise in his statement:

Science is the great antidote to the poison of enthusiasm and superstition.

By developing the inner faculties and powers through this book's many techniques, we can integrate, master and externalize the objective mind of a scientist, the heart of a Saint and the practicality of a businessperson for more sustained success and fulfillment.

The virtue of objectivity and practicality increases your performance to produce great results with certainty and converts your efficiency to effectiveness.

BENEVOLENCE IS ONE OF THE NOBLEST VIRTUES
The power to achieve happiness, contentment and right human relations and the key to accessing greater power
This virtue is expressed as being loving, kind and compassionate in a selfless way. Benevolence is a powerful tool to maintain right human relationships and is the key to being loved by many. This is one of the most powerful qualities in great inspirational leaders and motivators. It is a source of power for charismatic people. At first, a person utilizes the power of the heart energy center, the quality of personal love. Then after the person has developed spiritually and the top-of-head power center is active, the true quality of detached or selfless love starts to be expressed as benevolence. This virtue also has many ramifications like altruism, which will be discussed separately.

The absence of benevolence can create conflict and loneliness in life. Arthur Manning, our politician case study, is feared by his colleagues and tries to buy their loyalty with good salaries, and he is experiencing difficulties with his wife. Kristina Gunther, our very brilliant researcher case study, is too blunt in her communication and doesn't really enjoy interacting with people, preferring to be in her lab. One of her main challenges in life is loneliness.

So, how can we avoid these types of problems by developing benevolence fast or enhancing it further?

6 STEPS TO DEVELOP AND ENHANCE THE VIRTUE OF BENEVOLENCE

1. Start your day by expressing goodwill. Create and project good intentions and wishes to as many people as possible daily. Goodwill is the first rung in the ladder of success and the safety valve in the acquisition of power.
2. Avoid focusing on the negativity or mistakes of others and oneself.
3. Express benevolence through pleasant words and communications.
4. Practice the principle of forgiveness.
5. Express benevolence through active service and applied action.
6. Practice the spirit of fairness and a sense of justice.

Let's discuss the above steps in detail.

1. *Goodwill is the first rung in the ladder of success and the safety valve in the acquisition of power.*
   Goodwill expressed as good intentions is the seed of good actions, which when practiced regularly convert into good habits. A cultured personality is comprised of many good habits. Therefore, positive thoughts, pleasant wishes and right motives are a good way of building benevolence thoroughly.

Benevolence is not just an active way of expressing love or kindness, but is also abstinence from harmful thoughts, words and actions. Start and end your day with intentions of good-will. Humanity is starting to implement this virtue en masse.

The quality of thoughts and emotions that you radiate is what you'll receive back. Passion begets passion. Anger begets anger. Divine Love begets unconditional love.

Technique to Build Goodwill (5 minutes daily)

a. Spend 5 minutes right after you wake up to greet your day with gratitude for life and the source of your life. Use the feeling of the heart to express this for 1 minute.
b. Also silently express your good wishes to your family and loved ones, friends, co-workers and people whom you will be meeting throughout the day. Do this for 2 minutes.
c. Visualize or have the intention of a good and successful day and see your whole day's programs and goals achieved. If you have problems, visualize them being resolved properly. Focus more on the positive outcomes of your day (2 minutes).

2. *Avoid focusing on the negativity or mistakes of others and oneself.*
   If you want to avoid losing much time and energy, it is better to avoid contemplating too much not only the imperfections of others, but also your own weaknesses and mistakes. When there is a problem, you should focus more objectively on the solutions and lessons to be learned. Excessive analysis and evaluation of your negative tendencies can lead to guilt, anxiety, resentment or depression. And over-brooding on other people's faults can result in destructive criticism, anger or resentments. It is important to remember that no person has

perfect character and we are all capable of committing mistakes. Being mentally objective is important if you want to master this virtue of benevolence.

> *There is nothing wrong with green fruit.*
> *It is just waiting to ripen.*
> *Some people are like green fruit.*
> *They just need time to evolve,*
> *and evolution requires many processes,*
> *which implies more time.*

3. *Express benevolence through pleasant words and communications.*

    We are not born to please or agree with everyone. But there are ways in which verbal communication and the way of expressing things can be improved. I believe that people have to say what they really mean and mean what they say, but in the most appropriate, compassionate way. In the business world, some businesspeople compromise principles and values for financial profit and because of the doctrine that the customer is always right and needs to be pleased. Usually pleasing the clients and giving the best service are important procedures, but not to the extent that we compromise truth and values. For normal people, this sidetracking of virtues seems acceptable, but as a person evolves, righteousness and virtues cannot be compromised. Practice making a habit of verbally nurturing people while expressing the rightness of things sincerely and selflessly without having to always expect gains or rewards. This is true benevolence. Goodness begets goodness and without having to claim rewards, the law of nature fulfills itself to award what is due to you sooner or later.

Nurture others with positive, truthful words.
It doesn't cost anything to do so.
But mean what you say, and say what you mean.
Do it everyday. This is one of the most obvious
qualities of the most beloved leaders.
If you cannot be generous financially,
at least be generous with your words.

4.   Practice the principle of forgiveness.
The following old adage holds true:

To err is human and to forgive, divine.
Alexander Pope, English poet

Most people need to learn how to forgive and forget the negative past more, especially traumas and bad experiences. When people recall negative experiences and those who have hurt them, they go into a cycle of resentment and anger, which not only drains their energy, but also creates a negative emotional pattern that slows down their development and blocks their success. How do we accomplish this release from the past negativity? Try this.

YOU CAN RELEASE YOUR PAST NEGATIVE EXPERIENCES EASILY

As if this were the last day of your life, ask forgiveness from those who have been hurt by you and grant forgiveness to people who have hurt you or are still hurting you. You might want to make a habit of the following process monthly or periodically:

a. Briefly list the people who have been hurt by you, and highlight the lesson(s) behind it.

b. List the people who have hurt you or are still hurting you, and summarize the lesson(s) behind the problem.

c. Perform 3 sets of the **Synchronized Breathing Method.**

d. Close your eyes and imagine yourself in front of an ocean. Inhale and exhale slowly and relax. As you exhale slowly, externalize all negative feelings and thoughts about any relationship issues as if the ocean were absorbing these discomforts. Do this for about 3 minutes or until you feel better and calmer.

e. Visualize the people who have been hurt by you, one at a time, and mentally ask for forgiveness sincerely. Express inner apology and imagine yourself forgiven. Make a firm resolution not to commit the mistake again and imagine that the relationship is healed, reconciled or freed from disturbances.

f. Visualize the people who have hurt you or are still hurting you, and express your forgiveness to them, one person at a time, as if this were your last chance to do so. Mentally give your inner advice or comments objectively, and imagine them doing the right activities or learning the proper attitudes.

g. Mentally say the following affirmation at least 3 times:

> *I am a being of love and kindness. As I ask for compassion,*
> *I show compassion. As I ask for forgiveness from people*
> *whom I've hurt, I give forgiveness to anybody who has hurt me.*
> *Let all be completely forgiven. Let all be free. So it is!*

h. As much as possible, do all of the above processes a few times a week to make the new positive emotional and mental programs permanent.

i. Teach this technique to others if you think they would benefit.

TWO ASPECTS OF FORGIVENESS YOU SHOULD KNOW

There are two aspects of forgiveness: external and internal. Internal forgiveness is what we just finished as a process in the above technique, but the external aspect is a physical process. The violator should be informed or educated of the right attitude. If it is a violation of the law like a murder, then there should be justice and action to discipline the violator so the same mistake is not repeated. Also, physical, emotional and/or mental repair of the relationships – or a process of reconciliation – is almost always required. But first, it has to start with the good intention to forgive. When both external and internal forgiveness are achieved, then "forgetting" is also achieved spontaneously. When the problem is understood, detachment follows, and forgetting the negative experience and traumas of the past is experienced naturally.

5. **Express benevolence through active service and applied action.**

   Benevolence starts with positive motives and kind intentions, expressed as nurturing words, but it should be practiced through applied action. It can be actualized as:

   - Kind regards to others expressed as understanding, consideration and compassion
   - Helpfulness and selflessness accompanied with being mentally, emotionally and physically supportive to people and all species of nature
   - Establishing projects and services that help as many beneficiaries as possible
   - Selflessly motivating and inspiring other people and groups to become the best they can be

6. **Practice the spirit of fairness and sense of justice.**

   This is the key to inner satisfaction and inner peace. Being loving and kind is not enough to express benevolence. It has to be accompanied by fairness and the sense of justice to express the wisdom of the virtue fully. How can one test fairness and justice? There are man-made rules called social laws and codes of ethics that are temporal. There are also higher spiritual laws, universal truths and principles that are easy to grasp and implement by more advanced people. For average people, social laws and codes of ethics serve as their initial guidelines for fairness, but as a person evolves, the spiritual principles and universal truths should be their guiding laws. The major spiritual law is the Law of Karma or Cause and Effect: What you sow, you reap. It simply means that people have to be responsible and accountable for their thoughts, words and actions. This law can be used to create one's destiny in a positive way. One can predict one's future or destiny of groups, organizations or nations by studying what they are doing, observing and violating according to the Law of Cause and Effect. All of their past and present track records of good or bad ways will be harvested in the future. This is what we call predicting destiny with concrete reasoning.

A practical method to test fairness is to study the Golden Rule, one of the applications of the Law of Cause and Effect. This is a law of visible and invisible justice on thoughts created, words spoken and actions taken. The Law of Cause and Effect is expressed by two relevant subsidiary rules of the Golden Rule from ancient Chinese teachings and most religions. The Golden Rule, and its subsidiary rules, construct virtues, especially those of benevolence, altruism and justice. These rules can be applied through a process of role-reversal to express justice and fairness.

TWO ASPECTS OF THE GOLDEN RULE

Passive: DO NOT DO UNTO OTHERS WHAT YOU DO NOT WANT OTHERS TO DO UNTO YOU.

This will help guide people on what not to violate against others. Use this rule to validate and test the fairness of your decisions. This is a principle of abstinence or subtraction of negative tendencies.

Active: DO UNTO OTHERS WHAT YOU WANT OTHERS TO DO UNTO YOU.

This is a tool to be fair in implementing actions or solutions to problems. It is a reminder to take action to do good or express the right solutions to solve problems. It is a reminder to take active roles, to implement positive steps and to express virtues rather than just a mere abstinence from negativity.

These two aspects of the Golden Rule, as taught by Confucius, and the Law of Karma, when applied, can help solve even the biggest world problems or crises in humanity from the past, in the present and in the future. Some problems might take longer to solve when applying these rules and principles, but the solutions are more permanent and result in a fair or win-win process for all parties concerned.

As with almost anything in nature, there are exceptions to the rules when interpreted and applied incorrectly. There are universal subsidiary laws and principles to be employed along with the Golden Rule and Law of Karma for them to be a complete guide for one's life.

Additional Recommended Practices to Develop the Virtue of Benevolence

1. Daily, upon waking up, treat the day as if it were your last.
2. Make good intentions and wishes for as many people as possible, starting with your family and loved ones, co-workers, employer, subordinates and clients. Visualize the goodness developed in you and in everyone. This step activates your heart and top-of-head centers naturally. Do this for 2-3 minutes.
3. Be fair to everyone the whole day. Role-reversal or putting yourself in the shoes of others when making decisions, solving problems or negotiating is a good practice and habit to maintain fairness.
4. Be detached to the good things you've accomplished before they build up the ego. Do your duties as well as possible, spontaneously, without expecting fame, rewards or applause. Whatever you deserve will be rewarded to you in tangible or

intangible ways. The Law of Karma or universal Law of Cause and Effect fulfills itself whether you ask for it or not.

5. Periodically evaluate yourself. Do this monthly, with special evaluation on your birthday and at the end of the year. Do the following steps: List things that violate or harm people through your thoughts, words, habits or attitudes. Make a firm resolution to correct them and make sure you check yourself constantly not to repeat the same offenses.

6. Visualize or create the intention that you are already expressing the right attitude(s). This step requires repeated visualization to program your consciousness to instinctively express the proper behavior in the future.

7. Open your heart and let harmlessness be your natural state. The true requirement of the mastery of personal powers is harmlessness.

Greater powers are permanently achieved
through the virtues of benevolence and harmlessness.
When you have attained a level where even if you are pushed
to your limits, you will not misuse power,
then true personal powers are at your disposal.

When the heart and top-of-head centers are active and spiritually open, a person becomes more inclusively loving and harmless. Therefore, activating these power centers through meditation or breathing techniques is an important path for the mastery of power.

8. Do the Synchronized Breathing Method with extended inhalations and exhalation focusing on the **heart**, **mid-brow** and **top-of-head** power centers (5 minutes, 3 times weekly).

Altruism is Your Key to Financial Freedom
The key and power behind prosperity and sustained abundance

To be altruistic is not just being generous at the financial or material level, but also at the spiritual, mental, emotional and energy levels and in a more unconditional, unselfish way. At first, people are
generous with some hidden selfish intentions in the back of their
minds. This is excusable and understandable in ordinary people
because they are still "spiritual children" whose solar plexus center,
the lower desire center, is bigger than their heart center. When the
heart power center is active and functional, as in more advanced
mystics or loving people, the emotional instinct of being altruistic is
already a habit. The higher form of altruism is developed when the
top-of-head center is active and functional wherein the person gives
unconditionally at the material, emotional, mental and spiritual levels. These people express generosity as a sense of duty or a natural responsibility to others, humanity or the world, like many
wealthy people who support philanthropic work. Altruism is a habit
of highly developed people.

Altruism is expressed naturally by advanced Souls, Saints and
Sages because of a long-standing habit of generosity. Abundance in
life is not only measured in financial and tangible material assets, but
also in many intangible ways like good health, happiness, peace of
mind, smooth-sailing projects and life's fulfillment. There is such a
thing as invisible prosperity gained through the habit of altruism. It
can be called good luck or good karma of entitlement. The good
karma generated through generosity can be converted and harvested through different channels. It is a matter of where this good luck
or karma of abundance will go or defining how it will be received.
As mentioned earlier, good luck and the ability to be entitled to
good things go to the people who work for them.

Without altruism, some people may experience bad luck. Oscar
Wayne, the Olympian-turned-real estate businessman in one of our
case studies, started out with many advantages, but suffered a string
of accidents and health issues before recognizing the need to
express more altruism in his life. By putting his wealth into the serv-

ice of supporting orphans, his luck changed, and he achieved more balance, success and fulfillment as a result.

There are different levels of expressing generosity and altruism, starting from the merely physical and material levels. When people are financially generous, they tend to become wealthy. Financial and material prosperity are usually the result of not only hard work, but also generosity and abstention from stealing and unfairness. Hard work is not enough to make a person or organization successful and prosperous or to sustain abundance for a long time. There is also a need for intelligent disciplined work. Intelligent disciplined work equals hard work in a well-organized manner with right timing, plus good karma of entitlement.

The speed of achieving goals and removal of obstacles is directly related to the amount of karmic entitlement available to the individual or organization.

The inherited prosperity of many wealthy families and lineages was earned by their ancestors who practiced some of these principles of entitlement. But when their descendants cease to be generous, the flow of prosperity is terminated. Much inherited wealth in families and corporations fades away because of this. Therefore, it is wise to pass to the next generation or successions of leadership the virtue of altruism as the key to sustained abundance. Islam and Judaism tend to implement the law of tithing or appropriating a percentage of income for donations to the needy. Most of their members uphold and apply this principle of giving regularly, and this explains why many are super-rich and continue to enjoy abundance.

Taoism and Christianity also encourage altruism in their membership, but not with as much strict discipline as Islam and Judaism. Currently, many business organizations and wealthy individuals are becoming more generous, appropriating large sums of financial support for the needs of the world. They practice philanthropy not just for the benefit of tax exemptions for their donations, but they also feel a sense of responsibility for human development.

The individuals, corporations, organizations and nations who will be wealthy or who will sustain their abundance will be those who practice altruism. This is the key to sustained prosperity, and it is the principle of good luck and entitlement.

Many spiritual teachers recommend donating an average of 10% of your net earnings. Although charity begins at home and in the neighborhood, it is recommended to extend generosity globally. I think the altruism of the United States, Switzerland, Germany, Canada and other wealthy countries is the foremost key to their sustained prosperity aside from their technological and business advancements, hard work and persistence. These countries are also home to many generous people and groups. And in the corporate world, some of the companies who pay their workforce lucratively, have made their leaders and managers millionaires and are support-ing community projects are the most successful wealthy organiza-tions today. Bill Gates and his wife, Melinda, have donated a total of $24.9 billion (54% of his wealth) for philanthropic work as of December 1, 2003[21], more than the sum total of the other top 49 philanthropists in the world. Do we wonder why he is the richest person on earth today with almost $50 billion to his name?

How Can We Practice the Virtue of Altruism Better?
Those who have financial challenges need to practice this virtue more than those who are already prosperous. If one does not have this habit of generosity or if one just gives once in a while, here is a recommendation.

TECHNIQUES FOR PRACTICING THE HABIT OF ALTRUISM

1. *Form the habit of giving financially to a good cause.*
   Determine the cause or project that stimulates your compassion and give donations monthly. Start with an amount that's comfortable for you according to your budget. When the habit of generosity is formed after a few months, increase the amount of tithing to 5-10% of your net income after tax. The more you need to increase your income, the more you need to give. It takes some time for most people to form good habits. It is a good idea to put dates for your monthly donations and amounts in your planner or calendar as a fixed reminder. It is better to start small than never; therefore, start giving or sharing whatever you can as soon as possible.

2. *Evaluate your rewards of giving.*
   Observe the difference in your life, materially and spiritually, when you give a lot versus when you give little or do not give at all. This can be both experimental and experiential for you. Experiment over a few months to prove the principle of generosity. Practice the virtue and be patient to wait for the results. The law proves itself like the laws of physics, mechanics and gravity. Whether one understands them or not, the natural laws fulfill themselves. This is true of the virtue of altruism fulfilling its cause and effect under the Law of Karma. Be scientific and patient. Do not expect the return on your karmic investment immediately. When you plant corn, you don't harvest the next week, but once you harvest after a few months, the reward is given many-fold. The law of giving generously does not follow the Law of Subtraction, but rather the Law of Multiplication of investment returns on the donation.

3. *Teach the virtue to others.*
   After a few months of practicing generosity and having

proven it successful, teach it to others. Start with your family, including your children, and do it with your organization. Altruism is a good value to sustain your family's fortune or a company's continuous profitability.

Technique To Maximize Altruism

People who have been practicing the virtue of altruism as a way of life can still enhance its expression further as follows:

1. *Give what you need most.*

   Altruism is not just on the material or financial levels. You can also give and receive emotional, mental and spiritual benefits. Many people are rich financially and materially, but are not in good shape spiritually and in relationships. When people need more respect and love, they should give more respect and love.

   > *The thing that you need most*
   > *is the thing that you need to give most.*

   Here's a simple strategy to give what you need most:

List aspects and attributes you need the most	Individuals or projects you can contribute to that need these aspects or attributes

Make a schedule and strategy to practice altruism based on the above list. When? Immediately and constantly.

2. *To whom do you give?*

Invest your donations in the right cause with the right purpose. Giving and tithing should be done wisely and properly. Donate where there is maximum benefit.

Plant good seeds in the most fertile ground.
Invest donations in the same way.

HOW TO CHOOSE WHERE TO DONATE FOR MAXIMUM BENEFIT

1. Determine what individual projects or world causes can maximize your donation or tithing.

   Maximum benefit in harvesting good karma goes to a donation that has the greatest influence on world evolution and human development for the longest period of time and for the largest number of beneficiaries, human or otherwise.

2. Give to people, groups or organizations that have helped your life directly. Every year, make a list of people or organizations you can include in your practice of altruism. The amount of tithing is directly proportional to the help given to you and the necessity of the individual or organization.

3. Invest in good karma through donations before your need arises. It is easier to concretize your goals if there is entitlement to achieve them. This entitlement is lubricated by the good favors you've given to the people or organization involved in the project, but foremost is the good karmic account you've invested in ahead of time. That is why when people receive things beyond their expectations, we say they are fortunate. This is connected to the good luck or good fortune mentioned earlier as invisible prosperity. List those areas

of life you need to enhance and invest your donations in a related world necessity as follows:

PERSONAL REQUIREMENT	AREAS TO INVEST DONATIONS
Family success and future of children	Projects or organizations that help families, orphans or children
Good health	Projects or research on health and enhancement of health for others and humanity
Enlightenment and mental development	Work and projects on enhancement of education and scientific research
Good relationships	Research and projects on the improvement of human behavior, quality of life and resolution of conflicts, including works of the United Nations and its non-governmental organizations
Spiritual growth	Projects and organizations that help with the inner development and transformation of humanity
Beauty and attractiveness	Projects that clean and beautify the environment and those improving the arts

Oscar Wayne, our case study who brought more balance to his life through more philanthropic work, is an excellent example of applying the principle of donating what you need most. His parents sent him away to a boarding school at a very young age. This early sense of separation as a child contributed to many of his negative and destructive attitudes and habits as an adult.

By choosing to support an orphanage when he finally realized the value of altruism, he was able to give more children a better childhood than he had, and, thus, he could heal his own issues of separation and entitle himself to a happier, more fulfilled life.

Self-interest in the return on your good karmic investments is not against altruism. It is an intelligent way of using resources to be able to receive more in order to have more resources to give. As long as the intentions are good and the self-interest is not hurting people, groups, organizations or the world, it is not classified as selfishness. It is still considered a virtue.

OTHER LEVELS OF ALTRUISM

Living life is not just about material success and financial reward. As one evolves, practice and integrate all the levels of altruism as follows:

1. *Emotional altruism:*
   Nurture people with good and pleasant feelings and expressions of emotional kindness. Utilize love, compassion and understanding as tools. Do it daily to as many people as possible. This is one of the key qualities that would help Kristina, our brilliant researcher case study, have a happier, more balanced life.

2. *Mental altruism:*
   Sharing good ideas with others is the key to mental enlightenment and the good karma of receiving better ideas. If you want to receive new higher ideas, release the old ones as well

as the new ones that you have mastered and let others benefit from them. Teaching others the topic you want to master is the key to becoming an expert on the subject matter. Mentally nurturing and motivating others to become better is also an expression of this mental altruism. Even good intentions and wishes mentally created or expressed are considered mental altruism.

3. Spiritual altruism:

The key to rapid spiritual growth is to be spiritually generous to others. Supporting people to grow spiritually and facilitating their ability to comprehend their life's lessons and fulfill their lives is an expression of spiritual generosity. Giving advice on spiritual values and wisdom to others, especially to those who need timely help, is recommended. Therefore, supporting good religious projects or spiritual mentors and their organizations to spread teachings to transform and enlighten humanity is a great duty and service, which is usually the responsibility of more advanced people.

Another example is to be compassionate and forgiving to people or organizations who cannot fulfill their financial obligations to you, as in the case of bad debts. Not only will you forgive and cancel the loan if it is impossible to be paid, but perhaps you will help people or organizations recover. This might be too much for some people, but this virtue can be applied more easily by more evolved souls.

One thing I'll never forget as an example of this virtue is a man I met in Cali, Colombia. His teenaged son was in a final championship bicycle race, but before the last lap, a man murdered the son. It took the father a few months to recover from this trauma, but one day he regained his spiritual sense and internally forgave the murderer. He later found out that the killer, who was put in jail, also had a teenaged son. The father of the murdered boy visited the murderer's son and offered him his dead son's bike. He proposed to train him for the next bicycle race. The murderer's son won the bicycle race the next year with this gentleman's help and coaching.

How big is that heart and how strong the courage to implement the true Christian spirit that if they throw stones at you, throw them bread? This is spiritual altruism at work.

THINGS TO AVOID TO UNBLOCK THE FLOW OF PROSPERITY

- Do not delay cash flow or withhold what is due to others.
- Do not look down on lesser people like the poorer segment of society.
- Avoid pride. The lesson of pride is to be humbled, including in financial status.
- Avoid excessiveness and fanaticism. Rich people and big corporations go bankrupt when they violate this principle. It is natural that as you climb the ladder of fame and success, overhead expenses also increase – most of the time exponentially. But know your limits and always save, not only for the present, but also for the rainy days.

The virtue of altruism is first formed by small doses of generosity until it can automatically express as greater altruism up to the emotional, mental and spiritual levels. Like any other attitude, it takes a good reason to develop it and a lifetime to master, but it is never too late to do it, so practice the concepts immediately. Make the positive intention today and the action to do it follows.

> *We make a living by what we get;*
> *we make a life by what we give.*
> Winston Churchill, British Prime Minister

Group Consciousness is the Real Power Behind Big Success
The big key to sustaining power and achieving bigger goals in less time

One of the most important requirements for thriving in this highly competitive modern society is the ability to work in an effective team or with a powerful group. This is true in a family, business or spiritual service. With group work, bigger goals can be achieved in less time than if projects are done individually. There are also plans and missions that require many different talents and skills not often all expressed by one person. Behind the great success of any organization or leader is a group or team that made it happen. A great leader can achieve the so-called impossible with a powerful team. Group consciousness is a must in the working and development of effective teams, sustained success and personal influence.

What Do You Require to Develop Group Consciousness?

- The spirit of interdependence and coexistence
- The spirit of cooperation
- Proper skills and aptitude
- Right attitude
- Proper communication
- Inspiration
- Discipline
- Dispassion and detachment
- Group love and compassion

Let's discuss each requirement in detail.

The spirit of interdependence and coexistence

Through the spirit of interdependence and coexistence, one realizes that one cannot exist without others, that the true nature of life and creation is characterized by co-existence. When this is understood, then the true understanding of group work and group consciousness starts to flourish.

The real freedom is not in being independent
from your need of others,
but in knowing that your life exists because of others.

Nature expresses this idea of interdependence and co-existence through its ecosystem, and the whole of humanity needs to learn this principle to attain world peace and the right distribution of resources. With objectivity and humility, this principle is easy to understand.

The spirit of cooperation

Before people want to cooperate, they first need to know the goal and purpose of the undertaking; that the project and work are worth the investment of their time, talent and effort; and that it is aligned to their purpose or goals in life. Therefore, a person has to determine the ultimate objective of the project and that it does not violate values or established codes of ethics. It is best that the individual group members know the expected results of the project from the outset.

Proper skills and aptitude

The talents and qualifications of the cooperating person should fit the requirements and expectations of the group and leader. This will ensure that the individual member does not become a liability to the group. Developing the group's required aptitude and skills to accomplish the best-quality result is the responsibility of the leader and so with every member.

Right attitude

Whereas aptitude development requires the member to have skills and talents, the attitude requirement is more of the right psychological and spiritual behavior towards the goal and within the group or team process. Although the members need to cooperate wholeheartedly to make the execution of the plans and strategies easier, the right attitude does not imply that cooperation is always "yes, sir", "yes, ma'am" behavior. The right attitude involves more of a freedom to express creative ideas and clear communications properly and appropriately as long as these proposals are reasonable and do not delay the projects and negate results.

Once the group decision is made, everyone has to cooperate, respect the final decisions and fully implement the plans without setbacks and antagonism over their personal preferences. Fanaticism and excessiveness should be avoided, and objectivity and practicality should be employed.

Proper communication

This is one of the most important aspects of group consciousness for teamwork to succeed. All the visions and goals have to be known and communicated clearly to the members of the group, guided with a set of clear rules and protocols. The roles and job description of the leaders and members have to be properly communicated, preferably written in a coherent and integrated manner. Openness and integrity in the communication process are a must and have to be implemented wisely. Results and performance should be monitored with reports. The group has to be organized with schedules. Whether a group is small or large, it always requires targets and schedules, including deadlines. It is expected that members are accountable and trained with initiative and a mature sense of responsibility. Members should know the consequences of achieving and not achieving targets and deadlines.

Inspiration

Whether dealing with a short-term or long-term plan, groups perform better when they are inspired, happy and enjoy what they are doing. It is not only the leader who is responsible to make the group happy or inspire every member. Each group member should do their best to stimulate inspiration and the sense of joy in the group. Leaders can maintain inspiration in the group by helping everyone understand that each member's work or contribution is important, that the members make a big difference and that the group's result is justified by each member's effort. The group members and leaders should focus more on the end result and solutions rather than problems if they arise. It is expected that plans may encounter obstacles, opposition or delays. The important thing is not to dwell on the negative issues, but rather to pass through them courageously and objectively. A group is tested not in good times but in bad times. The group has to have a plan and contingency for possible problems to avoid surprises. In bad times, inspiration and will-power are needed most.

Discipline
To ensure that the group succeeds, discipline is a must among members. It is the one quality of a group that can make it succeed; its absence makes the group fail. Even talent, inspiration and good communication do not function without discipline in the group. The most disciplined teams are the most effective groups, and they usually have constancy of effort and great performance. The leader must lead by example by being disciplined.

Dispassion and detachment
When a group becomes fanatical, excessive or very emotional, the team can't function properly. In this case, the virtues of dispassion and detachment are needed. The members should not focus on personal likes or dislikes and should subordinate their individual preferences to the good of the group. Any disturbing and disrupting agenda brought by anger, jealousy, envy, violence, fear, separativeness and stress should be minimized or overcome immediately by the group or the leader. These negative energies should not be allowed to stay and grow in the group. The role of the leader and senior members of the group is to dismantle these poisonous qualities immediately. The training of the group members should include how to switch to the mental levels and exercise detachment whenever stressful and critical emotional situations arise. Being in the

mental state, focusing on the next step and keeping the group mind focused on the long-term goals are important protocols to develop dispassion and detachment.

Group love and compassion

Each member should be considered the other member's keeper. There should be friendship and love for the other members, but not passionate or sentimental love. Why? Because too much emotionalism imbalances the group rather than binds it. The loving relationships should be colored with professionalism and integrity, and at times impersonality in relationships should be practiced if required. The more mental and advanced members can do this more easily than the rest. But it is a practical future requirement for all members involved in teamwork. The true virtue of group consciousness is starting to develop in some groups and business organizations, but most groups and teams are still too emotional, sentimental and sometimes fanatical.

The requirements for the virtue of group consciousness just mentioned are simplified versions, but they can probably help some groups and their leaders who are still using a dictatorship style. A new process of co-creativity and conscious teamwork has to be developed. Other groups need to balance their excessive devotion to the leader with a more mental attitude and objective aptitude. Some spiritual groups need to incorporate a more practical quality of group work, and many materially- and commercially-oriented teams or groups have to taper their excessive money-oriented strategies to be guided by more environmentally-friendly and spiritual goals. Whether you are a businessperson, educator, politician or religious leader, the virtue of group consciousness is a necessary ingredient to sustain power and achieve bigger goals in less time. All the spiritual values and virtues discussed earlier are required to master the virtue of group consciousness. It is one of the last virtues to be mastered, but once developed, one becomes unstoppable even in the path of material success and spiritual evolution.

VIRTUE OF SACRIFICE: YOU NEED IT TO BECOME A LEGEND
The key to greatness and powerful service

In sports, politics, business, family or any endeavor, the virtue of sacrifice stands out as one of the keys to achieving great things and expressing a powerful life of service. Big sacrifices lie behind every great success: sacrifices of time, energy, effort, hard work, health and sometimes one's personal preferences. But distorted extreme sacrifices for materialism create the compromising of virtues at the expense of one's own or other people's well-being.

> *The consumption society has made us feel that happiness lies in having things, and has failed to teach us the happiness of not having things.*
>
> Elise Boulding, American peace activist

Great spiritual figures in world history like Jesus the Christ had to sacrifice their lives to embody the spiritual principle of love. The Buddha had to sacrifice his comfort as a prince to become an ascetic in order to unfold the virtue of wisdom. Martin Luther King's life was relinquished for the sake of civil rights. All the great leaders, heroes and saints are masters of this virtue. To leave a legacy, one needs this virtue. It is the bottom line of greatness. The best chess players are those who understand the principle of sacrifice in the early stage of the game in order to win at the end. This principle is partially stated as follows:

> *One-half of knowing what you want is knowing what you must give up before you get it.*
>
> Sidney Howard, American dramatist

The team that has a better chance of winning exerts extra miles of effort, energy and time in preparation compared to other teams. The principle of sacrifice is not what most people think. It is not relinquishing something bigger or greater for nothing or lesser. True sacrifice should not be seen as a trigger to suffering. In fact, it is a cause of joy or bliss. It is usually giving up a penny for a hundred dollars. Sacrifices almost always deserve greater rewards of contentment, joy and a feeling of greatness.

How can one start to relinquish lesser preoccupations in order to achieve greater things? The letting go of less important stuff – material, emotional, mental and even so-called "status" and beliefs – for the sake of greater goals and causes. Giving up unproductive activities to do more important work and service contributing to society or world need is a noble idea that older Souls do out of habit. But sacrifice is not martyrdom. It is selflessness and service-orientedness, but intelligently applied. It can be systematically implemented with the following:

7 STEPS TO INTELLIGENTLY APPLY THE VIRTUE OF SACRIFICE

1. Determine and list your most important goals in life that are the highest priority. Include the amount of time, resources, effort and attention you need to make them very successful monthly or yearly.
2. List all the less important goals and activities that can be reduced, relinquished or terminated in order to have more time, resources, energy and focus for your priorities. Implement the screening process immediately.
3. Determine your physical, emotional and mental attitudes and aptitudes that block or disrupt your effectiveness to achieve the important goals. Implement the changes, adjustments or reversals immediately.
4. Identify your personal desires and preferences that need to be relinquished or changed because they are not supportive

of your new priorities. These may include relationships or passions for a thing in the past that has sentimental value. Great personal sacrifices require courage, determination and commitment. This is where many people fail. They are very attached to the past, temporary possessions or relationships.

5. The ultimate reason, greater good and benefits of your goal – personal or for the good of humanity – constantly have to be remembered and focused upon to justify the reason for sacrifice. This is important for the individual or team.

6. People who do not have this virtue yet should start practicing by sacrificing smaller items within their capabilities. As it becomes a habit, then bigger things can be relinquished for greater goals.

7. The reward of being able to serve a great cause that contributes to life and society should justify the sacrifice, not just financial reward or fame. Many rewards supersede money and glory. These can include leaving a legacy and "spiritual monument" of greatness. Not all of the most remembered and revered beings of world history had publicity or money to achieve greatness. Many have exemplified the virtue of sacrifice and service to humanity. The good news is that we can do it too and it is never too late.

It is always good to bear in mind that mastery of this virtue of sacrifice is mastery of true leadership and greatness. It is the power behind greatness.

Service is an expression of inner growth and development. It is the muscle-building for virtues. It is also a barometer of inner development and spirituality.

Your Good Health Is A Barometer Of Your Success And Self-Fulfillment

The key to attaining and enjoying lasting success and fulfillment

Most people have never considered that good health is a virtue. Therefore, I am obliged to declare good health a virtue and one of the most important aspects of this book. All the other virtues are not easy to master and execute externally without good health. When one is sickly, will-power and vitality are more difficult to maintain even with techniques to master them.

When a person has cancer and is in pain, it is difficult to cooperate in a team or exercise discipline. It seems that when people are sick, mental and emotional power cease to function properly. Talents and educational degrees cannot be employed when people are bedridden or suffering with life-threatening diseases, so it should be clear that good health is one of the most important virtues. A wealthy person will understand their powerlessness when they are between life and death. Their titles, success and money do not mean much in the end. If you have undergone a near-death experience, you will understand what I mean.

Whether we are parents, business leaders, politicians, doctors, multibillionaires or spiritual leaders, we need to respect the law of health and consider the virtue of good health as an important aspect of sustaining success and fulfillment. Most success and leadership seminars focus too much on strategies for business skills and emotional and mental development, but do not address the maintenance of good health enough as a much-required attitude for success. Humanity has not yet realized this since vices that destroy health are still acceptable even among acclaimed leaders, brilliant people and even physicians.

For example, I know a super-wealthy and successful business leader who had a stroke at age 55 because of over-work, stress and vices and was bedridden with paralysis for many years. He said to me that his millions didn't mean much to him after that. I have had many successful wealthy people as clients who were the best in their field, but one day lost their health and were confined to their bed for the rest of their lives. Therefore, I can't over-emphasize the need to take care of your health.

Even many physicians with stressful lives and work still smoke and drink, and some of our well-known scientists and brilliant leaders are not the best examples of this virtue of good health. In fact, good health is not currently a priority of modern education compared to fame, money or career. No wonder many people don't take it seriously until they get really sick, which is sometimes too late.

If I had only...forgotten future greatness
and looked at the green things
and the buildings and reached out to those around me
and smelled the air and ignored the forms
and the self-styled obligations and heard the rain on the roof
and put my arms around my wife...It's not too late!

Hugh Prather, Author, lecturer, minister and counselor[22]

In the search for health and balance, it is wise not to be too preoccupied with success and pushing hard for fulfillment. Rather, true health comes from flowing with a healthy balance between introspection and being self-critical.

In the future, we will see that good health will be treasured
and considered a priceless gift equal to professional success.
Good health will be a demonstration and barometer of
spiritual maturity and a high culture.

How Do You Enhance Your Total Health and Well-Being?

Good health is not only the absence of physical ailments or discomfort; it is complete physical, emotional, mental and spiritual well-being. It is wholeness and balance of all aspects of a person. Since there is no one single solution on all the levels of health for now, we need to itemize levels of care of human bodies and consult different experts. The levels of care are:

- Physical health
- Vitality health
- Psychological health
- Spiritual health

Let's discuss each in detail.

Physical Level

Today physicians are still the most reliable experts with regard to the cure of physical diseases, although there are increasing numbers of new alternative medicine professionals who provide care for the physical body, including prevention of unhealthy conditions. Here are some general choices of currently available physical body care:

- For overall health, consult your physician, dentist, psychologist and healers periodically.
- For body structure and alignment problems, consult chiropractors and osteopaths.
- Try massage and other bodywork for combined physical and vitality work.
- Experiment as needed with other alternative healthcare like Oriental medicine, ayurveyda, homeopathy and energy healing.
- Consult with holistic nutrionists and other experts for a good diet. Spiritual teachers recommend a vegetarian or semi-vegetarian diet for advanced spiritual practices.
- For physical body fitness training, get a fitness coach or consultant.

- Martial arts training, especially internal martial arts like *tai chi*, *chi-gong* or *aikido*, provide energetic training more than just physical training. The Internal Stamina Exercise from chapter 4 is highly recommended.

Depending on your physical body condition and requirements, you may choose from the above recommended body maintenance methods. It is still recommended for each individual to be responsible for managing their health by:

- Sufficient rest and relaxation
- Recreation
- Proper diet and nutrition
- Removal of all vices. Consult experts on cessation of smoking, alcoholism and recreational drug use. If possible, avoid prolonged exposure to people with vices.
- Proper exercise and breathing techniques
- Proper physical hygiene, including a clean physical environment

Vitality Health

Vitality is the fuel of your physical body; therefore, it directly affects your physical health. By maintaining high vitality constantly, your ability to overcome stress and disease is better.

RECOMMENDED PRACTICES FOR YOUR VITALITY HEALTH

(3 times weekly)

1. Internal Stamina Exercise
2. Synchronized Breathing Method
3. Combination breathing or slow abdominal breathing
4. Make sure you get enough fresh clean air daily and, as much as possible, a few minutes of sun in the morning, which will help revitalize your aura. If possible, ventilate your house or workspace and expose them to sunlight.

5. Take natural supplements to detoxify and revitalize yourself. This combination is what I use for myself:

- Blue-green algae or barley grass: For detoxifying
- Psyllium products: For colon cleansing
- Red Korean or Chinese ginseng: For revitalizing effects
- Royal jelly: For revitalizing effects
- Bee pollen: For revitalizing effects
- Coral complex: For body strength and density

Different brands have different recommended dosages and frequency of use.

Psychological Health

Psychological health depends on a combination of emotional and mental health conditions. We live in an ocean of emotional and mental vibration; therefore, this invisible energy environment also affects our health. The people we work with and those who live with us also affect our emotional and mental health. Therefore, it is more complicated than just keeping ourselves emotionally and mentally clean. The city we live in is also stressed and polluted with many types of contamination, including negative vibrational energies.

TECHNIQUES TO MAINTAIN YOUR PSYCHOLOGICAL HEALTH

1. *Maintain high vitality.*
   Maintain high vitality constantly through exercise, breathing techniques, sufficient rest and proper food. It is easier to overcome all the surrounding pollution if your energy is high and your stamina is better.

2. *Release your stress.*
   Release stress and maintain a balanced emotional and mental positive attitude. Today, stress is so prevalent in modern life that people are getting used to it. It is affecting our health

negatively whether one notices the side effects or not. Stress weakens the immune system, drains physical, emotional and mental energy and lowers productivity and performance. It is a common weakness in most people, even very successful people. Before stress overwhelms you, let's correct or prevent it immediately:

   a. For quick release, use the **Synchronized Breathing Method** for 5 minutes daily.

   b. For long-term solutions and to remove the side effects in your body, do the Internal Stamina Exercise for 5-10 minutes, 3 times weekly or daily as required.

3. *Do the MDP Inner Renewal Meditation.*

Heal your emotions and mind for inner peace and to remove fears, phobias and negative psychological influences. Do the MDP Inner Renewal Meditation, 2 times weekly (see Chapter 8, pages 241-245).

4. *Purify the energy of your living and working environment.*

Purify your work and living space by burning sandalwood or palo santo incense. If you observe almost all religions, incense is used to purify their temples or worship areas. Even yogis use incense, especially sandalwood, to energetically clean stress and negative vibrations from their meditation room. You may also use the Chantrams of Transformation CD (available from MDP Global Resources at www.mdpglobal.com), which utilizes special sacred chants that transform the energy of the listener and the immediate environment.

5. *Enjoy a salt-water bath regularly.*

Have a salt-water bath to ease you whenever you are heavily stressed, very emotional or fatigued. Mix 1 cup of salt (regular salt) per 2 gallons of lukewarm water. Adding 10 drops of lavender oil will increase the healing effect of this therapeutic bath. Submerge yourself totally for 15-20 minutes before rinsing with soap and water.

6. Awaken the faculties of your emotions and mind.

Equip your emotions and mind with more advanced faculties, and continuously study and engage in productive social and mental activities. Keep the emotions and mind alive and active. Use them for service. Be futuristic.

Spiritual Health

This aspect of life can be enhanced by practicing your religion or other spiritual techniques properly. This book offers some practical methods for improving character, purifying your auras and power centers and enhancing inner faculties and virtues for a new systematic approach to spiritual growth. Doing service for a good cause helping human development and contributing to world evolution is a must if you want to accelerate your spiritual development.

To maintain your spiritual health as a way of life, you need to include:

- Continuous study of universal principles and spiritual subjects
- Applied service corresponding to your spiritual development
- Meditation and spiritual practices as a source of inner connections and power
- Proper development and use of faculties and personal powers for the greater good
- Participation in group work for human and world development. The more advanced a person becomes, the more spiritual health encompasses and integrates all the other aspects of health. In fact, at higher levels of inner training, physical, vitality, emotional and mental health are subordinated to spiritual goals and purpose.

The virtue of good health will increasingly
become a priority of the incoming culture
because it will be the gauge of the quality of life
one has lived. Good health will be a
demonstration of inner development and balance.

We have studied many principles through spiritual values and the concepts and methods by which they are acquired or achieved. This chapter contains a lesson for a lifetime for most people. It is important to know that great world evolution has been achieved little by little through these constant positive small steps that have endured the test of time. The same with your personal evolution – the positive change can be slow, step-by-step. But with these new organized strategies, why not develop faster and integrate different techniques instead of a linear approach? Let's change the old concept of linearity. Let's be synchronized. Master as many techniques as possible with the right discipline guided by right rhythm.

How Can You Get Started?
We'll make it simple and straightforward:

1. **Implement the strategies.** First, you've gone halfway there already with the concept and technical knowledge of deliberately and rapidly developing all the required aptitudes and attitudes for total performance. A strategy has already been provided; it's yours to implement.

2. **Study the eight core virtues deeply.** Revisit this chapter, and identify which aspects are your priorities and the immediate important needs that make a big difference in your life. The principles have been discussed in the most practical way possible as systematic procedures and techniques, which you can implement as a weekly practice. Master one or two virtues simultaneously every month and continuously develop them every year. Start with the virtues you need most.

3. **Write a schedule.** List in your planner or calendar your immediate priorities and create a realistic schedule for your chosen practices with dates, times and rhythm to do them, or you can follow the general schedules in chapter 9 on Practical Weekly Schedules, pages 247-259. This is part of implementing the virtue of discipline and constancy.

4. **Practice regularly.** Commit to practicing them regularly. Proficiency comes with practice, practice, practice, and results are inevitable.

5. **Teach these inner values to others.** It is also advisable to gradually introduce these spiritual principles to your family members, friends, associates or organizations. Start with receptive people you interact with regularly.

The higher quality of sustained success leading to greater self-fulfillment needs more than just right attitudes and aptitudes. It requires a constant willingness and ability to grow and to keep on going through the school of life whatever it brings.

KNOW YOURSELF:	DEVELOP YOURSELF:
Rate your current level of development of the 8 core values. Rate 0 to 4.	Where would you like your development of 8 core values to be in 6 months? Rate 0 to 4. Choose the top 3 values that would most dramatically improve your performance, success and fulfillment.

KNOW YOURSELF	DEVELOP YOURSELF
Discipline and constancy _____	Discipline and constancy _____
Will-power and vitality _____	Will-power and vitality _____
Objectivity and practicality_____	Objectivity and practicality_____
Benevolence _____	Benevolence _____
Altruism _____	Altruism _____
Group consciousness _____	Group consciousness _____
Virtue of sacrifice _____	Virtue of sacrifice _____
Good health _____	Good health _____

TOP 3 PRIORITY VALUES:

1. _____
2. _____
3. _____

The game of life can be lost at the finish line if people are not on guard until the very end of their lives. The single most important factor that brings the highest value to success is the spiritual virtues. They are the most important keys that set apart merely successful people and fulfilled human beings. At the end, self-fulfillment is a by-product of self-mastery. Consider this:

Knowledge through the mind brings success.
Wisdom through virtues brings fulfillment.

May you enjoy this higher path of your life!

CHAPTER 8

A MEDITATION TO HEAL
AND EMPOWER YOUR LIFE

◆

The MDP Inner Renewal Meditation™ expresses many of the applications and techniques to develop your faculties and virtues further. By practicing this meditation, your ability to integrate and balance the Success and Fulfillment Triangle — willpower, love and creative intelligence — is enhanced rapidly, safely and naturally. It is the synthesis of these three qualities that allows life's balance and self-fulfillment to come through easily. You may adopt it as your regular spiritual practice at least three times weekly or, if you do other practices for inner development, you may follow the weekly schedules recommended in chapter 9, Practical Weekly Schedules, pages 247-259.

MDP INNER RENEWAL MEDITATION
(3 times weekly): Available on CD at www.mdpglobal.com
BENEFITS:

- For deep relaxation, peace of mind and stress management
- For inner empowerment and spiritual development
- For enhancing your emotional and mental aptitudes and attitudes
- For purifying, unblocking and rejuvenating your different auras
- For improving relationships and healing your past

- For activating the expression of virtues and to integrate the faculties of will-power, love and creative intelligence in your life

PROCEDURE

A.   *Proper posture*

1. For this meditation, the best posture is to sit on a chair with your feet flat on the floor and your hands in your lap. You may also lie down as long as you keep your back aligned.
2. Close your eyes.

B.   *Inner purifications and breathing: Select any item (numbers 4-14 below) that concerns you.*

1. Start with the inner purifications. Free yourself from any physical, emotional and mental negativities or discomforts.
2. Imagine yourself in front of an ocean. What is important is your intention.
3. Breathe deeply and slowly and relax. During exhalation, have the intention to breathe out your negativities and discomforts.
4. Inhale deeply and breathe out to the ocean any discomfort, tension or pain in your body. Do it many times. Let the ocean absorb the discomforts and impurities (1 minute).
5. Inhale deeply and breathe out to the ocean stress or emotional pain and discomfort. Let the ocean absorb these negativities (1 minute).
6. Inhale deeply and breathe out irritability, anger or hatred. Let the ocean absorb the negative emotions (1 minute).
7. Inhale deeply and breathe out depression, boredom or frustrations. Let the ocean absorb them (30 seconds).
8. Inhale deeply and breathe out fears, guilt and worries. Let the ocean absorb the negative emotions (30 seconds).
9. Inhale deeply and breathe out resentment and anxiety. Let the ocean absorb these negative emotions (30 seconds).
10. Inhale deeply and breathe out any remaining negative feelings

and emotions. Let the ocean absorb all of the negativities (30 seconds).

11. Inhale deeply and breathe out harmful thoughts against anyone or any being. Let the ocean absorb the negative thoughts (30 seconds).

12. Inhale deeply and breathe out any mental limitations and blockages. Let the ocean absorb the negative thoughts (30 seconds).

13. Inhale deeply and breathe out any tendencies of excessive criticism, control and manipulation of others. Let the ocean absorb all of the negative tendencies (30 seconds).

14. Inhale deeply and breathe out anything that limits your freedom or obstructs your inner development. Let the ocean absorb any obstacles (30 seconds).

15. Relax and enjoy your new emotional and mental well-being.

C.   Opening and activating the heart center

1. Now, be aware of your heart center at the center of your chest. This is an area where you can experience love, inner peace and inner joy. Inhale deeply and exhale slowly while being aware of the area at the center of your chest (1 minute).

2. As you breathe, silently affirm:

I am a peaceful, loving and joyous person.

Repeat it 7 times as you continue breathing slowly. Create this wonderful feeling of love, joy and peace within you. Express your love, gratitude and respect to your family, loved ones and those who have helped your life.

3. Visualize yourself being more loving and caring to other people and their needs. Start with your family and loved ones. Express love to your friends. Express good wishes and respect to your co-workers. Mentally ask for forgiveness from people who have been hurt by you. Also, forgive the people

who have hurt you. Experience the love, peace and joy within you.

D. *Activating your mental stamina and intelligence*

1. Focus on your mid-brow center between your eyebrows and breathe slowly for 1 minute. By breathing while focusing on this center, you can enhance the ability to think more clearly and properly. Inhale deeply and exhale slowly as you mentally say 3 times:

> *I am a creative and intelligent person.*
> *I will use my creativity and*
> *intelligence lovingly and properly.*

E. *Opening and activating the top-of-head power center for spiritual faculties and to align with the Soul*

1. Focus on the center on top of your head and breathe slowly for 1 minute. By breathing while focusing on this point, you can enhance the ability to acquire more inspiration, divine understanding and wisdom. Inhale and exhale slowly and mentally say 3 times:

> *I respect the divinity within myself.*
> *I respect the divinity within All.*
> *I respect the greatness of the Supreme Source of Life.*

2. Relax and let go. Enjoy the inner peace and stillness (2 minutes).

F. *Absorption and circulation of internal energy*

1. To assimilate the internal energy and vitality, breathe slowly while focusing on your navel. (1 minute)

2. To further improve the absorption of energy, concentrate on your palms and soles of the feet as you inhale and exhale slowly for 30 seconds.

G. *Blessing service* (2 minutes)

I. With intention, share some of your positive and loving energy and vitality with your loved ones, friends and anyone who needs help. You may use the following affirmation many times for at least 2 minutes:

> *I humbly offer myself as an instrument to share love, peace, joy, beauty, creativity, truth and goodwill with my family, loved ones, friends and co-workers. So it is!*

Now open your eyes and smile.

After getting what we want in life, achieving almost all our goals yearly and becoming very accomplished, one thing we probably don't need is the stress that comes with success. And what we might require most to enjoy the fruits of our labor are peace of mind, a clear conscience and a complete sense of well-being. This meditation has helped many successful professionals and executives achieve this state of inner fulfillment. Use it every week; then it is yours to say, "Life is so good! I am balanced and fulfilled"!

CHAPTER 9

PRACTICAL WEEKLY SCHEDULES

◆

Maximizing your personal and professional life is an excellent idea to sustain greater and long-lasting success, but walking the path to self-fulfillment is the ultimate goal. Satisfying your life in the five important areas – Family and Home, Career and Work, Social Life and Environmental Contribution, Health and Recreation and Spiritual Life – brings balance to material and spiritual life, which is only a dream for most people today, but a reality for those who incorporate the teachings of this book. By applying the principles, practical tools and inner values of this book, you can achieve greater breakthroughs in life, leading you to physicalize your vision, mission and plans faster and more effectively. It's a valuable investment and lifetime pursuit for anybody who wants to be ahead. This is especially so for leaders, executives and professionals who want to stay on top of their lives with greater usefulness, success and capacity to serve.

The weekly schedules in this chapter have been designed to offer you integrated strategies and tools for:

- ◆ Constant vitality, good health and greater will-power to succeed
- ◆ Enhanced emotional intelligence and magnetism for right human relations
- ◆ A sharper mind with integrated concrete and abstract mental faculties

- Advanced leadership faculties with inspirational, intuitive and visionary powers
- Developing right attitude, aptitude, wisdom and inner values to transform success into self-fulfillment
- Balance of material and spiritual life

RECOMMENDED WEEKLY PROGRAMS

Daily Goodwill Programming

5 minutes every day anytime, but preferably immediately after you wake up and before you start your day. You can also do this technique before you sleep. Refer to chapter 7, page 203.

Internal Stamina Exercise: 5-10 minutes (pages 75-86)
Goals:

- Rejuvenate and revitalize your body quickly
- Release your stress and tension
- Enhance your metabolism and accelerate weight loss
- Oxygenate your blood and detoxify your body
- Enhance your total health and well-being

This can be practiced daily or as per the basic weekly schedule listed on pages 252-253.

Synchronized Breathing Method: 5-10 minutes (pages 96-98)
Goals:

- Quick stress management
- Purify and calm your emotions and mind and boost your vitality quickly
- Rejuvenate your human energy system fast
- Stimulate divine connection and increase Soul energy flow to your personality

This can be practiced daily or anytime you need to detoxify and revitalize. This breathing method is one of the most useful techniques supporting other practices.

Inner Purification and Revitalization Breathing Techniques:
5-10 minutes (pages 153)
Goals:

- Release your stress and negative psychological conditions
- Increase your vitality and improve your stamina fast
- Enhance your concentration and mental focus
- Improve your health and well-being

This can be done anytime you need to release internal blockages and boost your vitality. It can be performed in combination with the Synchronized Breathing Method.

Nostril-Controlled Breathing:
5-10 minutes (pages 99-102)

- A few minutes deliberately breathing through one nostril at a time to balance your gentleness (left nostril) and dynamism (right nostril). This inner balance brings internal well-being and a sense of wholeness.

SPECIAL ADDITIONAL PRACTICES: (optional)

- *Will-power enhancement* Use any method that suits you. Refer to chapter 7, Will-power Enhancement Techniques (pages 188-193)
- *Pure thinking time and mental aptitude development and application* (chapter 6, pages 176-177) Allocate at least 1-2 hours weekly to develop your mind, especially the abstract mental faculties, or practice the different mental power appli-

cations. Your thinking time should not only focus on your career. It should include all five areas of life. It is recommended to involve higher study of new spiritual subjects that are of immediate interest for your next step. This is very important for mental muscle-building and a requirement for integrating your concrete and abstract mental powers.

MDP Inner Renewal Meditation: 30-40 minutes (pages 241-245)
Goals:

- Develop your different energy auras
- Inner purification and revitalization of your human energy system
- Activation of your different mental, emotional and vitality faculties
- Improve the connection of your personality to the power of your Soul
- Healing of relationships and past negative tendencies
- Spiritual service through blessings

This meditation can be practiced anytime you need healing on any level.

Continuous Study and Aptitude and Attitude Development:

- Invest in time to read and apply this book and other educational materials weekly. Also listen to CDs and watch DVDs for any specific information you need to learn for your next step.
- Attending courses and seminars is an excellent investment that adds value towards continually supporting your success and ability to stay at the top of your life.

Study and Practice of Spiritual Virtues: (Chapter 7)

- This is an indispensable aspect of the integrated path of success and fulfillment.
- Select and practice weekly the inner values that you need most.

Periodic Self-Auditing:

- On pages 256-260, you will find blank versions of the Know Yourself-Develop Yourself assessments you have used throughout this book. You can copy these pages to evaluate yourself every six months so you can continue the habit of doing current self-assessments and setting ongoing development targets.

SUMMARY OF WEEKLY SCHEDULES
Culturing yourself for greater success and fulfillment:
  I. For initial training: I year

	AM/PM	Monday	Tuesday	Wednesday	Thursday	Friday	Saturday	Sunday
Goodwill Programming	AM	5	5	5	5	5	5	5
	PM	min						
Internal Stamina Exercise + Combination Breathing	AM	5	5	5	5	5	5	5
	PM							
	AM	5		5		5		
	PM							
Synchronized Breathing + Nostril-Controlled Breathing	AM							
	PM	5		5		5		
	AM							
	PM	10		10		10		
Inner Purification Breathing + Will-Power Development	AM							
	PM		5		5			
	AM							
	PM		10		10			
Inner Renewal Meditation	AM						40	
	PM							
Pure Thinking Time	AM							
	PM							60
Book/Audio/Video Study	AM							
	PM		45	45	45			
Time Invested Weekly	AM	15	10	15	10	15	50	10
	PM	15	60	60	60	15		60

TOTAL: **AM** – 2 hours, 5 minutes in the morning
           PM – 4 hours, 30 minutes in the evening

II. For healthier and more advanced practitioners or after 1 year of Level I

	AM/PM	Monday	Tuesday	Wednesday	Thursday	Friday	Saturday	Sunday
Goodwill Programming	AM	5	5	5	5	5	5	5
	PM	min						
Internal Stamina Exercise + Combination Breathing	AM	5	5	5	5	5	5	5
	PM							
	AM	5		5		5		
	PM							
Synchronized Breathing + Nostril - Controlled Breathing	AM							
	PM	5		5		5		
	AM							
	PM	10		10		10		
Inner Purification Breathing + Will-Power Development	AM							
	PM		5		5			
	AM							
	PM		10		10			
Inner Renewal Meditation	AM						40	
	PM							
Pure Thinking Time	AM							
	PM							120
Book/Audio/Video Study	AM							
	PM		60	60	60			
Time Invested Weekly	AM	15	10	15	10	15	50	10
	PM	15	75	75	75	15		120

TOTAL: **AM** – 2 hours, 5 minutes in the morning
PM – 6 hours, 15 minutes in the evening

The spiritual principles and methods in this book are similar to the laws of physics or mathematics; when you use them, the corresponding results are foreseeable and measurable by your increased productivity at work, your enhanced relationships everywhere you go, your deepening true inner values, the change towards greater perspective in life and your increasing capacity to serve selflessly.

Expertise and great results in any chosen endeavor almost always go to those who master the basics. Therefore, I recommend that you understand and regularly practice the fundamentals in this book. The right integration and synergy of the different techniques as listed in the tabulated weekly schedules make the strategies powerful, resulting in positive inevitable results.

What makes a martial arts expert an expert is
practice, practice, practice!
But what makes a martial arts master a master
is not just continuous practice,
but ceaseless practice guided by wisdom.
This is also true of the champion in life,
the totally fulfilled person.

May this book and its teachings light your path to a happier, healthier and fuller life, guiding you to continually build a lasting legacy of service to your family, profession, community, humanity and the world.

Best wishes on your path from success to fulfillment!

Know Yourself-Develop Yourself Forms

5 Most Important Areas of Life Assessment and Goals

Know Yourself:
Current Time Allocation in 5 Areas of Life

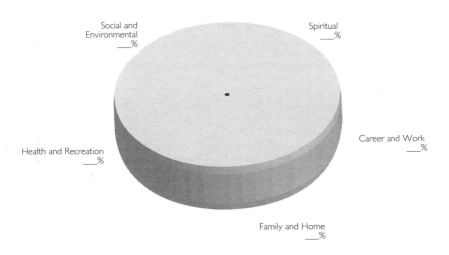

Social and
Environmental
___%

Spiritual
___%

Career and Work
___%

Health and Recreation
___%

Family and Home
___%

Develop Yourself:
Targets for the next 6 months: Time Allocation in 5 Areas of Life

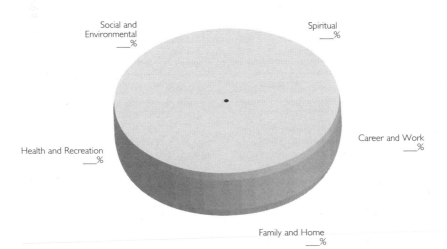

Social and
Environmental
___%

Spiritual
___%

Career and Work
___%

Health and Recreation
___%

Family and Home
___%

SUCCESS AND FULFILLMENT TRIANGLE ASSESSMENT AND GOALS

KNOW YOURSELF-DEVELOP YOURSELF KEY

4 = Fully developed
3 = Well developed
2 = Partially developed
1 = Just starting to develop
0 = Not developed at all

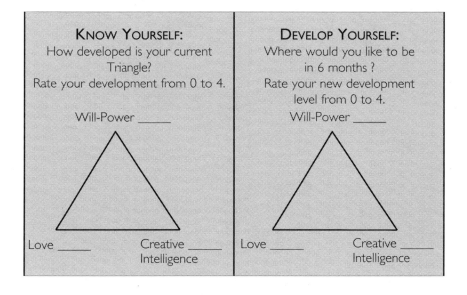

KNOW YOURSELF:
How developed is your current
Triangle?
Rate your development from 0 to 4.

Will-Power _____

Love _____   Creative _____
                    Intelligence

DEVELOP YOURSELF:
Where would you like to be
in 6 months ?
Rate your new development
level from 0 to 4.

Will-Power _____

Love _____   Creative _____
                    Intelligence

ENERGY ANATOMY DEVELOPMENT ASSESSMENT AND GOALS

KNOW YOURSELF: Rate the level of development of your physical and energy anatomy components. Rate 0 to 4.	DEVELOP YOURSELF: Where would you like to be as your next step in 6 months? Rate 0 to 4.
Physical body ____	Physical body ____
Vitality ____	Vitality ____
Emotions ____	Emotions ____
Spiritual antenna/ inspiration ____	Spiritual antenna/ inspiration ____

EMOTIONAL INTELLIGENCE FACULTY ASSESSMENT AND GOALS

KNOW YOURSELF: Rate your current level of emotional intelligence qualities. Rate 0 to 4.	DEVELOP YOURSELF: Where would you like to be in 6 months? Rate 0 to 4.
Sense of inner peace and contentment ____	Sense of inner peace and contentment ____
Emotional instincts ____	Emotional instincts ____
Win-win outcomes sought in decision-making ____	Win-win outcomes sought in decision-making ____
Kindness, compassion and inclusiveness ____	Kindness, compassion and inclusiveness ____
Many friends and good relationships ____	Many friends and good relationships ____
Emotional magnetism ____	Emotional magnetism ____

MENTAL FACULTIES ASSESSMENT AND GOALS

KNOW YOURSELF: Rate your level of mental development. Rate 0 to 4.	**DEVELOP YOURSELF:** Check the top 3 mental faculties you want to focus on improving in the next 6 months.
Common sense	Common sense
High grade of common sense	High grade of common sense
Memorizing and storing information	Memorizing and storing information
Mental analysis	Mental analysis
Problem-solving and decision-making ability	Problem-solving and decision-making ability
Capacity to materialize goals	Capacity to materialize goals
Ability to organize and structure	Ability to organize and structure
Innovation	Innovation
Creativity	Creativity
Ability to visualize	Ability to visualize
Imagination	Imagination
Love-intellect faculty/ focus and awareness	Love-intellect faculty/ focus and awareness
Legendary vision and knowing your niche	Legendary vision and knowing your niche
Philosophical and principle-based thinking	Philosophical and principle-based thinking

8 CORE VALUES DEVELOPMENT ASSESSMENT AND GOALS

KNOW YOURSELF: Rate your current level of development of the 8 core values. Rate 0 to 4.	DEVELOP YOURSELF: Where would you like your development of 8 core values to be in 6 months? Rate 0 to 4. Choose the top 3 values that would most dramatically improve your performance, success and fulfillment.
Discipline and constancy _____	Discipline and constancy _____
Will-power and vitality _____	Will-power and vitality _____
Discipline and constancy _____	Objectivity and practicality _____
Objectivity and practicality _____	Benevolence _____
Benevolence _____	Altruism _____
Altruism _____	Group consciousness _____
Group consciousness _____	Virtue of sacrifice _____
Virtue of sacrifice _____	Good health _____
Good health _____	
	TOP 3 PRIORITY VALUES:
	1. _____
	2. _____
	3. _____

Quick References

---◆---

END NOTES

[1] Marketdata Enterprises

[2] Ibid

[3] Shakespeare, William. *The Life of King Henry the Eighth* [Wolsey at III, ii]

[4] Gelernter, David. "Bill Gates" in *Time 100: American Legends* (New York: Time Books, 2001) p. 85

[5] Ibid, p. 86

[6] Lemonick, Michael D. "Edwin Hubble" in *Time 100: American Legends* (New York: *Time* Books, 2001) p. 100

[7] Ibid, p. 99

[8] Ibid

[9] Kluger, Jeffrey. "Robert Goddard" in *Time 100: American Legends* (New York: *Time* Books, 2001) p. 97

[10] Schickel, Walter. "Walt Disney" in *Time 100: American Legends* (New York: *Time* Books, 2001) p. 66

[11] Blake, William. "Annotations to the Works of Sir Joshua Reynolds" in *The Complete Poetry & Prose of William Blake.* (New York: Anchor Books, 1988) p. 647

[12] Edler, Richard. *If I Knew Then What I Know Now.* (New York: Berkley Publishing Group, 1997) p. 72

[13] Gelertner, David. "Screen Saviors" in *Time 100: American Legends* (New York: *Time* Books, 2001) p. 87

[14] Matthiessen, Peter. "Rachel Carson" in *Time 100: American Legends* (New York: *Time* Books, 2001) pp. 105-107

[15] Huey, John. "Sam Walton" in *Time 100: American Legends* (New York: *Time*

Books, 2001) p. 82

16 Ibid, p. 80

17 Tannen, Deborah. "Oprah Winfrey" in *Time 100: American Legends* (New York: *Time* Books, 2001) p. 151

18 Ibid

19 Blake, William. "Auguries of Innocence" in *The Complete Poetry & Prose of William Blake*. Lines 1-4. (New York: Anchor Books, 1988) p. 490

20 Edler, Richard. *If I Knew Then What I Know Now.* (New York: Berkley Publishing Group, 1997) p.220

21 *Business Week.* "The 50 Most Generous Philanthropists." December 1, 2003.

22 Prather, Hugh. *Notes to Myself.* (New York: Bantam Books, 1983) p. 1

RECOMMENDED READING

The best results in our lives come through balancing whatever we choose to do. This is also true in book study and learning. In our present age of information explosion, it is not easy to determine which books are most useful. Many available resources can be either too theoretical or excessively materialistic in approach. The following are recommended for your study and research on topics to bring balance, success and fulfillment to your life:

I. PERSONAL AND BUSINESS GROWTH AND SUCCESS:

1. *The 100 Absolutely Unbreakable Laws of Business Success.* Brian Tracy (San Francisco, CA: Berrett-Koehler Publications, Inc., 2000)
2. *The 7 Habits of Highly Successful People.* Stephen Covey (New York, NY: Simon & Schuster, 1990)
3. Leadership books by John Maxwell (Nashville, TN: Thomas Nelson Publishers)
4. *Executive EQ.* Robert K. Cooper and Ayman Sawaf (New York, NY: The Berkeley Publishing Group, 1998)
5. *If I Knew Then What I Know Now.* Richard Edler (New York, NY: The Berkeley Publishing Group, 1997)
6. *The Successful Business Plan.* Rhonda Abrams (Palo Alto, CA: Running 'R' Media, 1991)
7. *The 7 Spiritual Laws of Success.* Deepak Chopra (San Rafael, CA and Novato, CA: Amber-Allen Publishing and New World Library, 1994)
8. *The Laws of Money, The Lessons of Life.* Suze Orman (New York: Free Press, 2003)

II. BOOKS FOR PRACTICAL SPIRITUAL REFERENCE:

1. *Inner Powers to Maximize Your Performance* - 2nd Edition. Del Pe (The Woodlands, TX: MDP Global Resources, www.mdpglobal.com, January 2003)
2. Books by Master Choa Kok Sui on Pranic Healing and Inner Sciences (Makati City, Philippines: Institute for Inner Studies, www.pranichealing.org)

MDP Organizations

Founded by Del Pe

GLOCEN® is an international organization specializing in services and programs that help executives, professionals, teams and organizations maximize performance and balance life. Its core philosophy applies Eastern wisdom and Western practicality to bring success and fulfillment in all areas of life.

GLOCEN offers seminars, coaching-mentoring-consulting, offsite retreats and career certification programs.

Seminars Series:

* Health, Vitality and Stress Management Strategies
* Aptitude and Attitude Development Strategies
* Success and Self-Fulfillment Strategies:
  - Family and Work Life Balance
  - Integrated Time and Life Management
  - 8 Core Values to Transform Success Into Fulfillment

Coaching-Mentoring-Consulting Services:

* Balancing Your Life Program
* Vitality and Stress Management Solutions Program
* Addiction/Vice Elimination Program for Executives
* Addiction/Vice Elimination Program for Families
* Strategies to Transform Modern Families
* Family Stress Management Program
* Maximizing Intimacy in Relationships Program
* Yearly Life Cycle Program for Professionals
* Mastering Time and Life Planning
* Urgent Crisis Management and Solutions
* Fast Decision-Making and Problem-Solving Program
* Aptitude and Attitude Development Programs
* Spiritual Mentoring for Success and Fulfillment
* Organizational "Corporate Healing" Programs
* Organizational Visionary Consulting Programs
* Inner Powers Martial Arts Program for Stamina, Will-Power and Instinct Development

Offsite Retreats:

- Health, Vitality and Stress Management Retreats
  - Addiction/Vice Elimination and Revitalization
- Aptitude and Attitude Development Retreats
- Success and Self-Fulfillment Retreats
  - Inner Renewal and Spiritual Journeys to Special Places
  - Family and Work Life Balance
- GLOCEN Career Development and Certification Retreats

ESOCEN® is a U.S.-based organization with international centers serving individual clients, families, groups and organizations with personal transformation, energy healing, holistic education and spiritual training. Its core philosophy is balancing material and spiritual life while accelerating inner development.

ESOCEN offers seminars, coaching-healing, retreats and career certification programs.

Seminars Series:

- Healing Science
- Family and Social Transformation
- Holistic Education for the New Generation
- Spiritual Training and Development

Coaching-Healing Services:

- Yearly Life Cycles
- Balancing Material and Spiritual Life
- Addictions/Vice Elimination
- Stress, Pain, Fatigue and Sleeplessness
- Hyperactivity, Attention Deficit and Aggression
- Women's Health Issues
- Healing Families at Risk
- Family Stress Management
- Vitality and Stress Management for Educators
- Inner Powers Martial Arts™

Mentoring Services:

- Family Transformation
- Holistic Education
- Inner Powers Development
- Spiritual Training

RETREATS:

+ Family Stress Management
+ Addiction/Vice Elimination and Revitalization
+ Inner Renewal and Spiritual Development
+ ESOCEN Career Development and Certification

MDP Global Resources® is a multimedia company producing products to help maximize personal and professional performance, enhance inner development and foster group consciousness. The company supports programs aligned with global transformation and advancement for humanity.

MDP Global Resources serves clients and organizations through:

+ *Inner Powers to Maximize Your Performance* book
+ *From Success to Fulfillment* book
+ MDP Inner Renewal™ Meditation CD
+ Chantrams of Transformation™ CD
+ MDP Namascar Meditation™ CD
+ Activating and Balancing Your Power Centers™ CD
+ Beat Your Fatigue and Stress Fast™ DVD
+ Body Therapy Exercises and Inner Powers Meditation™ DVD
+ Will-Power Development™ DVD
+ MDP Life Planner™

FOR FURTHER INFORMATION OR SERVICES

GLOCEN and ESOCEN conduct coaching, consulting, seminars and training programs in in-house and public venues in over 15 countries. Inner Renewal and Stress Management Centers in several countries provide ongoing support and nurturing for graduates and members. Our international team is dedicated to serving and assisting our clients on a personal and continuous basis after seminars or consulting engagements.

Please write or call:

P.O. Box 7947
The Woodlands, Texas USA 77387
Tel: 1-800-352-6014 ✦ 1-936-273-9153 ✦ Fax: 1-936-273-9230

GLOCEN: www.glocen.com   ✦ info@glocen.com
ESOCEN: www.esocen.com   ✦ info@esocen.com
MDP Global Resources: www.mdpglobal.com   ✦ info@mdpglobal.com